ELEGIAC FEELINGS AMERICAN

Also by GREGORY CORSO

The Happy Birthday of Death
Herald of the Autochthonic Spirit
Long Live Man

ELEGIAC FEELINGS AMERICAN
AMERICAN
GREGORY CORSO

A NEW DIRECTIONS PAPERBOOK

ACKNOWLEDGMENTS

Some of these poems first appeared in the following books and mag-
azines: *The Beats, Between Worlds, The Cambridge Review, Chelsea,
Combustion,* Death Press, *Evergreen Review, The Floating Bear,
Front Unique 2, Fuck You/a Magazine of the Arts, The Hasty Papers,
Kulchur* (Basic Books), *The Needle, New Departures, New Direc-
tions 19, Nomad, Of Poetry and Power* (Basic Books), *Olympia, The
Outsider, Quadrat-Prints* (Amsterdam), *Ramparts, Three Arts Quar-
terly, Two Cities* and *Yugen.*

New Directions wishes to thank Fernanda Pivano, publisher of the
first edition of "The Geometric Poem," for permission to reproduce
it in facsimile in the present collection. Copies of the original, signed
limited edition are available from the publisher, 14 Via Manzoni,
Milan, Italy.

Manufactured in the United States of America
First published as New Directions Paperbook 299 in 1970
Published simultaneously in Canada by Penguin Books Canada Limited
New Directions Books are printed on acid-free paper

New Directions Books are published for James Laughlin
by New Directions Publishing Corporation,
80 Eighth Avenue, New York 10011

FIFTH PRINTING

CONTENTS

ELEGIAC FEELINGS AMERICAN

ELEGIAC FEELINGS AMERICAN

for the dear memory of John Kerouac

1

How inseparable you and the America you saw yet was
never there to see; you and America, like the
tree and the ground, are one the same; yet how
like a palm tree in the state of Oregon. . . dead
ere it blossomed, like a snow polar loping the
Miami—
How so that which you were or hoped to be, and the
America not, the America you saw yet could
not see
So like yet unlike the ground from which you stemmed;
you stood upon America like a rootless
flat-bottomed tree; to the squirrel there was no
divorcement in its hop of ground to its climb of
tree. . . until it saw no acorn fall, then it knew
there was no marriage between the two; how
fruitless, how useless, the sad unnaturalness
of nature; no wonder the dawn ceased being
a joy. . . for what good the earth and sun when
the tree in between is good for nothing. . . the
inseparable trinity, once dissevered, becomes a
cold fruitless meaningless thrice-marked
deathlie in its awful amputation. . . O butcher
the pork-chop is not the pig— The American
alien in America is a bitter truncation; and even
this elegy, dear Jack, shall have a butchered
tree, a tree beaten to a pulp, upon which it'll be
contained—no wonder no good news can be
written on such bad news—
How alien the natural home, aye, aye, how dies the tree
when the ground is foreign, cold, unfree— The
winds know not to blow the seed of the
Redwood where none before stood; no palm is
blown to Oregon, how wise the wind— Wise

too the senders of the prophet. . . knowing the
    fertility of the designated spot where suchmeant
    prophecy be announced and answerable—the
    sower of wheat does not sow in the fields of
    cane; for the sender of the voice did also send
    the ear. And were little Liechtenstein, and not
    America, the designation. . . surely then we'd
    the tongues of Liechtenstein—
Was not so much our finding America as it was America
    finding its voice in us; many spoke to America
    as though America by land-right was theirs by
    law-right legislatively acquired by materialistic
    coups of wealth and inheritance; like the citizen
    of society believes himself the owner of society,
    and what he makes of himself he makes of
    America and thus when he speaks of America
    he speaks of himself, and quite often such a he
    is duly elected to represent what he represents. . .
    an infernal ego of an America
Thus many a patrioi speaks lovingly of himself when he
    speaks of America, and not to appreciate him is
    not to appreciate America, and vice-versa
The tongue of truth is the true tongue of America, and it
    could not be found in the *Daily Heralds* since
    the voice therein was a controlled voice,
    wickedly opinionated, and directed at gullible
No wonder we found ourselves rootless. . . for we've become
    the very roots themselves, —the lie can never
    take root and there grow under a truth of sun
    and therefrom bear the fruit of truth

Alas, Jack, seems I cannot requiem thee without
    requieming America, and that's one requiem
    I shall not presume, for as long as I live there'll
    be no requiems for me
For though the tree dies the tree is born anew, only until
    the tree dies forever and never a tree born
    anew. . . shall the ground die too

4

Yours the eyes that saw, the heart that felt, the voice that
        sang and cried; and as long as America shall
        live, though ye old Kerouac body hath died,
        yet shall you live. . . for indeed ours was a time
        of prophecy without death as a consequence. . .
        for indeed after us came the time of assassins,
        and who'll doubt thy last words "After me. . .
        the deluge"
Ah, but were it a matter of seasons I'd not doubt the return
        of the tree, for what good the ground upon
        which we stand itself unable to stand—aye the
        tree will in seasonal time fall, for it be nature's
        wont, that's why the ground, the down, the slow
        yet sure decomposition, until the very tree
        becomes the very ground where once it stood;
        yet falls the ground. . . ah, then what?
        unanswerable this be unto nature, for there is
        no ground whereon to fall and land, no down,
        no up even, directionless, and into what, if what,
        composition goeth its decomposition?
We came to announce the human spirit in the name of
        beauty and truth; and now this spirit cries out in
        nature's sake the horrendous imbalance of all
        things natural. . . elusive nature caught! like a
        bird in hand, harnessed and engineered in the
        unevolutional ways of experiment and technique
Yes though the tree has taken root in the ground the ground
        is upturned and in this forced vomitage is spewn
        the dire miasma of fossilific trees of death the
        million-yeared pitch and grease of a dinosauric
        age dead and gone how all brought to surface
        again and made to roam the sky we breathe in
        stampedes of pollution
What hope for the America so embodied in thee, O friend,
        when the very same alcohol that disembodied
        your brother redman of his America,
        disembodied ye— A plot to grab their land, we
        know—yet what plot to grab the ungrabbable

5

land of one's spirit? Thy visionary America were
impossible to unvision—for when the shades of
the windows of the spirit are brought down, that
which was seen yet remains. . . the eyes of the
spirit yet see
Aye the America so embodied in thee, so definitely rooted
therefrom, is the living embodiment of all
humanity, young and free
And though the great redemptive tree blooms, not yet full,
not yet entirely sure, there be the darksters, sad
and old, would like to have it fall; they hack
and chop and saw away. . . that nothing full
and young and free for sure be left to stand at
all
Verily were such trees as youth be. . . were such be made
to fall, and never rise to fall again, then shall
the ground fall, and the deluge come and wash
it asunder, wholly all and forever, like a wind
out of nowhere into nowhere

2

"How so like Clark Gable hands your hands. . ." (Mexico
conversation 1956) —Hands so strong and
Mexican sunned, busy about America, hands I
knew would make it, would hold guard and
caring
You were always talking about America, and America
was always history to me, General Wolfe lying
on the ground dying in his bright redcoat
smittered by a bluecoat hanging in the classroom
wall next to the father of our country whose
heart area was painted in cloud. . . yes, ours
was an American history, a history with a
future, for sure;

How a Whitman we were always wanting, a hoping, an
        America, that America ever an America to be,
        never an America to sing about or to, but ever
        an America to sing hopefully for
All we had was past America, and ourselves, the now
        America, and O how we regarded that past!
        And O the big lie of that school classroom! The
        Revolutionary War. . . all we got was
        Washington, Revere, Henry, Hamilton, Jefferson,
        and Franklin. . . never Nat Bacon, Sam Adams,
        Paine. . . and what of liberty? was not to gain
        liberty that war, liberty they had, they were the
        freest peoples of their time; was not to *lose* that
        liberty was why they went to arms—yet, and
        yet, the season that blossomed us upon the scene
        was hardly free; be there liberty today? not to
        hear the redman, the blackman, the youngman
        tell—
And in the beginning when liberty was all one could hear;
        wasn't much of it for the poor witches of Salem;
        and that great lauder of liberty, Franklin, paid
        100 dollar bounty for each scalp of the wild
        children of natural free; Pitt Jr. obtained most of
        the city of brotherly love by so outrageous a
        deception as stymied the trusting heart of his
        red brother with tortuous mistrust; and how
        ignorant of liberty the wise Jefferson owning the
        black losers of liberty; for the declarers of
        independence to declare it only for part of the
        whole was to declare civil war
Justice is all any man of liberty need hope for; and justice
        was a most important foundling thing; a diadem
        for American life upon which the twinship of
        private property and God could be established;
How suffered the poor native American the enforced
        establishing of those two pillars of liberty!

From justice stems a variable God, from God stems a
           dictated justice
"The ways of the Lord lead to liberty" sayeth St. Paul. . .
           yet a man need liberty, not God, to be able to
           follow the ways of God
The justness of individual land right is not justifiable to
           those to whom the land by right of first claim
           collectively belonged;
He who sells mankind's land to a single man sells the
           Brooklyn Bridge
The second greatest cause of human death. . . is the
           acquiring of property
No American life is worth an acre of America. . . if No
           Trespassing and guarding mastiffs can't tell you
           shotguns will
So, sweet seeker, just what America sought you anyway?
           Know that today there are millions of Americans
           seeking America. . . know that even with all
           those eye-expanding chemicals—only more of
           what is not there do they see
Some find America in songs of clumping stone, some in
           fogs of revolution
All find it in their hearts. . . and O how it tightens the heart
Not so much their being imprisoned in an old and
           unbearable America. . . more the America
           imprisoned in them—so wracks and darkens the
           spirit
An America unseen, dreamed, tremors uncertain, bums the
           heart, sends bad vibes forth cosmic and
           otherwise
You could see the contempt in their young-sad eyes. . . and
           meantime the jails are becoming barber shops,
           and the army has always been
Yet unable they are to shave the hurricane from their eyes
Look unto Moses, no prophet ever reached the dreamed of
           lands. . . ah but your eyes are dead. . . nor the
           America beyond your last dreamed hill hovers
           real

8

3

How alike our hearts and time and dying, how our America
out there and in our hearts insatiable yet
overflowing hallelujahs of poesy and hope
How we knew to feel each dawn, to ooh and aah each
golden sorrow and helplessness coast to coast
in our search for whatever joy steadfast never
there nowever grey
Yea the America the America unstained and never
revolutioned for liberty ever in us free, the
America in us—unboundaried and unhistoried,
we the America, we the fathers of that America,
the America you Johnnyappleseeded, the
America I heralded, an America not there, an
America soon to be

The prophet affects the state, and the state affects the
prophet— What happened to you, O friend,
happened to America, and we know what
happened to America—the stain. . . the stains,
O and yet when it's asked of you "What happened to him?"
I say "What happened to America has happened
him—the two were inseparable" Like the wind
to the sky is the voice to the word. . . .
And now that voice is gone, and now the word is bone, and
the America is going, the planet boned
A man can have everything he desires in his home yet have
nothing outside the door—for a feeling man, a
poet man, such an outside serves only to make
home a place in which to hang oneself
And us ones, sweet friend, we've always brought America
home with us—and never like dirty laundry, even
with all the stains
And through the front door, lovingly cushioned in our
hearts; where we sat down and told it our
dreams of beauty
hopeful that it would leave our homes beautiful

And what has happened to our dream of beauteous
America, Jack?
Did it look beautiful to you, did it sound so too, in its cold
electric blue, that America that spewed and
stenched your home, your good brain, that
unreal fake America, that caricature of America,
that plugged in a wall America. . . a gallon of
desperate whiskey a day it took ye to look that
America in its disembodied eye
And it saw you not, it never saw you, for what you saw was
not there, what you saw was Laugh-in, and all
America was in laughing, that America brought
you in, brought America in, all that out there
brought in, all that nowhere nothing in, no
wonder you were lonesome, died empty and
sad and lonely, you the real face and voice. . .
caught before the fake face and voice—and it
became real and you fake,
O the awful fragility of things

"What happened to him?" "What happened to you?" Death
happened him; a gypped life happened; a God
gone sick happened; a dream nightmared; a
youth armied; an army massacred; the father
wants to eat the son, the son feeds his stone,
but the father no get stoned
And you, Jack, poor Jack, watched your father die, your
America die, your God die, your body die, die
die die; and today fathers are watching their
sons die, and their sons are watching babies die,
why? Why? How we both asked WHY?
O the sad sad awfulness of it all

You but a mere decade of a Kerouac, but what a lifetime in
that dix Kerouac!
Nothing happened you that did not happen; nothing went
unfulfilled, you circ'd the circle full, and what's
happening to America is no longer happening

10

to you, for what happens to the consciousness
of the land happens to the voice of that
consciousness and the voice has died yet the
land remains to forget what it has heard and the
word leaves no bone
And both word and land of flesh and earth suffer the same
sick the same death. . . and dies the voice
before the flesh, and the wind blows a dead
silence over the dying earth, and the earth will
leave its bone, and nothing of wind will roll the
moan, but silence, silence, nor e'en that will
God's ear hear

Aye, what happened to you, dear friend, compassionate
friend, is what is happening to everyone and
thing of planet the clamorous sadly desperate
planet now one voice less. . . expendable as the
wind. . . gone, and who'll now blow away the
awful miasma of sick, sick and dying
earthflesh-soul America

When you went on the road looking for America you found
only what you put there and a man seeking gold
finds the only America there is to find; and his
investment and a poet's investment. . . the same
when comes the crash, and it's crashing, yet
the windows are tight, are not for jumping; from
hell none e'er fell

4

In Hell angels sing too
And they sang to behold anew
Those who followed the first Christ-bearer
left hell and beheld a world new
yet with guns and Bibles came they
and soon their new settlement became old
and once again hell held quay

The ArcAngel Raphael was I to you
And I put the Cross of the Lord of Angels
upon you. . . there
on the eve of a new world to explore
And you were flashed upon the old and darkling day
a Beat Christ-boy. . . bearing the gentle roundness of things
insisting the soul was round not square
And soon. . . behind thee
there came a-following
the children of flowers

North Beach, San Francisco, 1969

12

SPONTANEOUS REQUIEM FOR
THE AMERICAN INDIAN

Wakonda! Talako! deathonic turkey gobbling in the soft-
footpatch night!
Blue-tipped yellow-tipped red-tipped feathers of whort dye
fluffing in fire mad dance whaa whaa dead men red
men feathers-in-their-head-men night!
Deerskin rage of flesh on the bone on the hot tobacco
ground!
Muskhogean requiems america southeastern, O death of
Creeks, Choctaws,
The youthful tearful Brave, in his dying hand trout, well-
caught proud trout,
Softest of feet, fleet, o america dirge, o america norwegians
swedes of quid and murder and boots and slaughter
and God and rot-letters,
O pinto brays! O deatheme sled mourning the dying chief!
Berries, spruce, whortle, cranky corn, bitter wheat; o scarcity
of men!
High-throttled squawlark, sister warrior, teepee maid, scar
lover, crash down thy muskrat no longer thy flesh
hand and rage and writhe and pound thy Indianic
earth with last pang of love of love,
o america, o requiems—

Ghost-herds of uneaten left to rot animals thundering across
the plains
Chasing the ghost of England across the plains forever ever,
pompous Kiwago raging in the still Dakotas, o amer
ica—
America o mineral scant america o mineralize america o
conferva of that once
great lovely Muskhogean pool, o oil-suck america despite,
oil from forgetive days, hare to arrow, muskellunge to
spear, fleet-footed know ye speed-well the tribes
thence outraced the earth to eat to love to die,
o requiems, Hathor off-far bespeaks Wakonda,

heraldic henequen tubas whittled in coyote tune to mourn
        the death of the going sun the going sled of each
        dying, sad and dying, shake of man, the tremble of
        men, of each dying chief slow and red and leather
        fur hot—
Shake slow the rattler, the hawk-teeth, the bettle-bells,
        shake slow dirge, o dirge, shake slow the winds of
        winds, o feathers withered and blown,
Dirge the final pinto-led sled, the confused hurt sad king of
        Montanas,
Strike dumb the French fur trappers in their riverboat brool
        mockery, no chant of death in such a wealth of musk-
        rat and beaver, shun them,
O slam squaw hysteria down on america, the covered wagon
        america, the arrow flamed wagons of conquest, the
        death stand of quakers and white-hooded hags and
        proud new men, young and dead,
O Geronimo! hard nickel faced Washington Boliva of a
        dying city that never was, that monster-died, that
        demons gathered to steal and did,
O Sitting Bull! pruneman Jefferson Lenin Lincoln reddead-
        man, force thy spirit to wings, cloud the earth to air,
        o the condor the vulture the hawk fat days are gone,
        and you are gone, o america, o requiems,
Dry valleys, deathhead stones, high Arizonas, red sun earth,
        the sled,
The weeping bray, the ponymarenight, the slow chief of
        death, wrinkled and sad and manless, vistaless, smoke-
        less, proud sad dying—
Toward the coyote reach of peak and moon, howl of hey-
        day, laugh proud of men and men, Blackfoot, Mo-
        hawk, Algonquin, Seneca, all men, o american, peaked
        there then bow
Thy white-haired straw head and, pinto imitated, die with
        the rising moon, hotnight, lost, empty, unseen, music-
        less, mindless; no wind—

In the grim dread light of the Happy Hunting Ground
A century of chiefs argue their many scalps, whacking the
　　yellow strands of a child against the coaly misty
　　harsh of tent;
It falls apart in a scatter of strewn, away, gone, no more,
　　back free out of the quay, into the bladder seep of
　　the bald dead seeking the hairless rawhead child of
　　whiteman's grave;
O there is more an exact sorrow in this Indianical eternity,
Sure o america woof and haw and caw and wooooo whirl
　　awhirl here o weep!
Indianhill woe! never was the scalp of men the prime knife
　　in the heart of a savagengence era, Clevelandestroyer
　　of manland, o requiems,
O thundercloud, thunderbird, rain-in-the-face, hark in the
　　gloom, death,
And blankets and corn, and peaceful footings of man in
　　quest of Kiwago, america, Kiwago, america, corn
　　america, earthly song of a sad boy's redfleshed song
　　in the night before the peered head intrusive head of
　　laughing thunderbolt Zeus, o the prank, o the death,
　　o the night,
Requiem, america, sing a dirge that might stalk the white
　　wheat black in praise of Indianever again to be, gone,
　　gone, desolate, and gone;
Hear the plains, the great divide, hear the wind of this night
　　Oklahoma race to weep first in the dirge of mountains
　　and streams and trees and birds and day and night
　　and the bright yet lost apparitional sled,
The bowed head of an Indian is enough to bow the horse's
　　head and both in unison die and die and die and
　　never again die for once the night eats up the dying
　　it eats up the pain and there is no Indian pain no
　　pregnant squaw no wild-footed great-eyed boy no
　　jolly stern fat white-furred chief of tobacco damp
　　and sweet, o america america—

15

Each year Kiwago must watch its calves thin out; must
    watch with all its natural killers dead, the new
    marksmen of machines and bullets and trained stud-
    ied eyes aim and fire and kill the oldest bull, the king,
    the Kiwago of the reminiscent plain—
Each year Wakonda must watch the motionless desert, the
    dry tearless childless desert, the smokeless desert, the
    Indianlessadly desert—
Each year Talako must watch the bird go arrowless in his
    peace of sky in his freedom of the mouth of old
    america, raw wild calm america,
O america, o requiem, o tumbleweed, o Western Sky, each
    year is another year the soft football doesn't fall, the
    thin strong arm of spear never raised, the wise coun-
    cil of gathered kings no longer warm with life and
    fur and damp and heat and hotcorn and dry jerky
    meat, each year no squaw titters her moony lover of
    hard love and necessary need of man and wife and
    child child, each year no child, no mien of life, good
    life, no, no, america, but the dead stones, the dry
    trees, the dusty going winded earth—requiem.

Pilgrim blunderbuss, buckles, high hat, Dutch, English, pat-
ent leather shoes, Bible, pray, snow, careful, careful, o but
feast, turkey, corn, pumpkin, sweet confused happy hosty
guests, Iroquois, Mohawk, Oneida, Onondaga, Thanksgiving!
    O joy! o angels! o peace! o land! land land land,
    o death,
O fire and arrow and buckshot and whisky and rum and
    death and land,
O witches and taverns and quakers and Salem and New
    Amsterdam and corn,
And night, softfeet, death, massacre, massacre, o america,
    o requiem—
Log-cabins, forts, outposts, trading-posts, in the distance,
    clouds,
Dust, hordes, tribes, death, death, blonde girls to die, gowns
    of ladies to burn, men of redcoats and bluecoats to
    die, boys to drum and fife and curse and cry and die,
    horses. . . to die, babies. . . to die;

Yeeeeeeeeeeeeeeeooooooooooooo! Harrrrrrrrrrrrrraaaaaaaaaa!
EEEEEEEeeeeeeEEEEEEaaaaaaaaaaaaaah!
To die to die to die to die to die to die . . . america, requiem.
Corn, jerky, whortly, the Seneca in a deacon's suit, gawky,
    awkward, drunk,
Tired, slouched—the gowns and bright boots pass, the quick
take-your-partner-swing-to-the-left-swing-to-the-right hums
all is over, done, the Seneca sleeps, no sled, no pinto, no end,
but sleep, and a new era, a new day, a new light and the
corn grows plenty, and the night is forever, and the day;

The jetliner streams down upon Texas,
                    Requiem.

Motorcyclist Blackfoot his studded belt at night wilder than
bright hawkeyes sits on his fat bike black smelly brusqued
assy about to goggleeye himself down golden ventures whiz-
zing faster than his ancestral steed past smokestacks banner-
shacks O the timid shade of Kiwago now! the mad roar
exhaustpipe Indian like a fleeing oven clanking weeeeee
weeeeeee no feathers in his oily helmet O he's a fast engine
of steam zooming unlaurelled by but he's stupid he sits in
Horn & Hardart's his New York visit and he's happy with
his short girls with pink faces and bright hair talking about
his big fat bike and their big fat bike, O he's an angel there
though sinister sinister in shape of Steel Discipline smoking
a cigarette in a fishy corner in the night, waiting, america,
waiting the end, the last Indian, mad Indian of no fish or
foot or proud forest haunt, mad on his knees ponytailing &
rabbitfooting his motorcycle, his the final requiem the final
america READY THE FUNERAL STOMP goodluck charms
on, tires aired, spikes greased, morose goggles on, motor gas
brakes checked! 1958 Indians, heaps of leather—ZOOM
down the wide amber speedway of Death, Little Richard,
tuba mirum, the vast black jacket brays in the full forced fell.

MUTATION OF THE SPIRIT

. . . These poems all bear the same theme, yet each page is
a separate poem, and yet again each joins up to make a
whole poem. . . and the poems can be shuffled up and
read as chance would have it. . . . No one poem comes first
or last.

Last night a white apple fell from the loneliest tree in the
     world
Today the field is green the sun bright and warm
Children attend their spirits the old knit knit knit knit
Chicken cries Sacramental sobs from the chapel A window
     closes
Loneliness grandeur and blue lambs whorled eyes rinsed
     light
Swimming deer And now the long hike back to the city
Smells of rats and pasty poisons horizons of fuming domes
     dynamos
Vast sick sense smudgepots gasping black smoke
Cheese-cloth faces dead carts bells a white arm
A long pale arm falls across the port.
           •

Depression may relinquish all definitions
yet joy shall acquire precise usage
Frenzy may leave terms phrases and evacuate basic form
yet soundness shall keep the senses specialized
Imperfection may discredit the odd the rare
yet shall perfection honor the typical
Blemishes humiliate the outlandish the unique the strange
yet excellence extols the orthodox the natural
Adornment seduces the odious
yet severity restores the loveable
Garnishment mayest ravish the vile.
Festooning mayest shanghai the accursed
may seize the nauseating the foul the beastly
may rape the unspeakable
Yet shall bareness liberate the estimable

18

Direction breakthrough meteorological panic
        cloud-cover thermotemperature
I am prepared to believe that drama of sky
Give it clear I can hear
It's no longer When will I break through this dream
        suddened upon me by questioning life
no longer is it A life unquestioned
        did well enough unquestioned
No the signals are clear I can hear
        and I can ask
        Who is that man whose snip-snap
        makes him more than that mark madcap
        Please who is he tell wild salvo
Nintoku emperor of Japan nay
        Germanicus so loved by his soldiers
BREAK hovers the Visigoth
like a great blonde-fuzz moth
o'er the flickering lamp of Rome
OUT and darkness is home
        Barbs and Vandals axed whatever light remained
        It was a time of paganblack candles
        and they glowed only when it rained
Soggy and despair damp S P Q R drenched quaestor
        woeful omen'd air
little white gowned rose girl
        broken on the spoor
O lions O falcons and snakes S is axed from P
        and Q from R is tore
Without Rome stout men with mastiffs hold justice
My words led a thought through them
and saw the back of justice.

Dusty Bright nee Fleshy Bright airey hermaphrodite is
     he-she spirit
is to the sun what the sun is to the earth the sun's sun yet
     Dusty Bright is nothing light
Light takes form is thin is round is fat is long but spirit is
     the shape and size of faith
Like a blind man led by an eyeless dog the measure of faith
     is the competence of the dog
Dusty laughs at the sun-addict who hails the sun as
     abundant as all-giving as IT
She being pure spirit is closer to it thus knows better she
     damns the sun as tight
as a spark-pincher and accuses it of being more hateful of
     her than it is of night
How much longer will it be before Miss Bright-Mr Bright
     reaches across the sky's circuit
and with Betsy Ross-like scissors snips the light too long the
     sun's puppet
Quick let us quickly promote Dusty Bright ere the denied
     Measure take flight
and become agent to the unlight of deathics the nightest
     night leaving all our spirits a doubt of air tailored
     for voidical fit
Come Spirit Bright Light nee Fleshy Bright alias Dusty
     Bright
Come adorned in sun foliage in the final mutation in this
     God-closed age

Outside where suns are there is no light
I've my back to the dawn
Ahead is black
Ahead are agents cleaning their guns
Suddenly at the window a whorl of burning snow
          Cold Cold thermotaurical wish of awful joy
Suns everywhere all over the place
But sunlessness is all I know
Come Standby spirit my spirit fails

          Some truththing has burst fake and cold upon me
I would out I would putter in the garden
But deathly dacthal like a micro-tornado chased me
Double-pulse back in O come to me my extra soul
All those shared decanters we so joyously drained
          Together we outsang the devil choir
To the core To the very innerspout a workhorse of a spirit
The Muse would throw it to God in Heaven like a ball
          Joy was in His slow relay I'd sneak a hundred looks
Down down into the sky I looked the Muse readied her
          catch
What seemed there churned the airey dark into light
Was her excited hands hands made of sun waiting
          to catch me

O there is burning snow flickering the air
and white velvet sloths in the falling sun
and flamewhite bears tip-toeing across the trees
and oh there are streams of luminous fish in mountain winds
and seldom beasts sinking in snowclouds
O zero zoo invisibility
whose naught were for its loss a hope true
yet truer for its futility

Sheep and jackmen wash in axes and flails
Dogchurch drops the sleeper
its gorgeous stained-glass fangs glow
in night in Ulan Bator Khoto walks a woman
dawn is sky sky is blue blue is long and far
her shadow falls the length of sky every Thursday
September she judges the earth October she stings the venial
November she slays the mortal December he is born fat
black is fat is thick is deep is brink death and sleep
white is thin is a losing man a slouched old woman
black weighs 10 hectograms white a gram

The field is green The sun is bright
Old men with wide pants hold twisted belts
and children attend their spirits
the vision was peace O how silly I was in that scene
Ether sirens and lights and loud numbers
Unborn ages wriggling shapes and cowels
Yesterday has become a century away
Meager valor of historic years away
Who wrings this piteous surrender of the spirit like a wet
       towel Don't say.

O walking crucifixes hooded and bowed
treking catacombic apothecaries
Grains drams and ounces of aphasia
Etherized Popes their desperado nods
raise welts of confessional memories on my lips
I speak
A desperate night and I set cry
to a sleeping angel's lips with a kiss
I speak what is demanded of one such as I
TRUTH ABOVE ALL the demand
I am a wreck of truth Damn such demand
I cried I would rather my value be true
than truth be my value
Smell of nuns
Trepidations of old Italian ladies
Omega in January rectified in February
To wake up and see my only friend
a wife who smells of delicious sleep
I kiss kiss kiss O not so bad life

It is past That world we saw alas in vain
Nor shall we look upon another like it again
Our closing eyes nothing will we remember
of those deathlight days made of December

The satyr is no such thing never a syrinx
        O cypresses O river maidens O jinx
The Arcadian shepherd is famished thin
a goat is all he has and it has eaten
a fatal pokeberry bush

Sirens of light Loud numbers
Unbronzed clay wrings the piteous surrender
of the spirit
like a wet towel

10 hectograms of black is night
Burning snow is in the air
Blue is long and far
its shadow falls skylength
        Autumn walks a woman
September her orange ambitions
October black courage.

The decencies of life have lost their way
Tamarinds seek phalangers to flay
Green-thumbed sprayers of dacthal
Scampering vermin
Darkness with all its failure annunciations stills the transept
Chip chip ecclesiastics aggregate in rhythmic throngs
Gods collide and eclipse the sick sun
What's seen What's seen
Eyes to the source and rinsed light between
Look upon look the great secret deep seen
Oracle and dial wand and radar
An angel comes and the new sun is not far
Arise new spirit unroll a nadir wool
From tip to top the source is measured full
The eternal exists as well in the ephemeral
Air is everywhere and life is changeable
In the yard of the old sun retired spirits sleep
Into the pool of night the swimmer of light leaps

O PLENITUDE O WEALTH FORTUNE CAPITAL
    SUBSTANCE
Gone flashing pity the merciful cries the surging hungers
Man's infinite soul-want passes through night like a scornful
    dream
What mystic promise has not been kept
       We've journeyed among the days of the future
       We've timed our eyes to petrify omens in flight
       We heard the spirit from Mars berate reactionary
          stars
       We learned that hopes of happiness exist beyond our
          sphere
          that all living intelligence is of good cheer
          of honesty without prevarication
          of prophecies free of gloom
       Everywhere here and way beyond there
          suns glow with accordant liberties
       Paradise even pervades Hell cleansing like a bell
       The final gong deafens the sacrosanct doom from its
          door
          from its halls its rooms Paradise evermore
          glowed with laughing liberties
       A hell-less universe is on its knees

Chark the Wlamptcor's Deathhymn
CHARK witchbrake CHARK
The child of the monoecious future shall be born of itself
O All Surround Around And Round In Between
Skullyell in the dispensary
      AROWAROO ARREE
Bat-searchyell beamhits from churchyardyell
To Belfryell
      BELLROW BELROO RREEBELL
How diwsalis the fiwk woaksalis
How torckfozo Wloadgow and Woskwozo
The infernal parachutejumper nods The bum of the Atlantic
    nods
Back and forth in slow pendulous noddery
All's TOCKROW TOCKROO TOCKRREE.

LINES WRITTEN NOV. 22, 23—1963
—in Discord—

So what's it like being an American Assassin this silly
    uncertain day?

Not I with chiromancerian eyes
    Do I raise my right hand that Popes halt
    Talmudians relent?
Like a table of fishy Chinamen
    I laugh my purpose into dopey disguise
Who'll see this
    or that
    or where-they're-at
bereft of such eyes?

> The Good   The Bad
> I seek the Good
> But *I Am* Good!
> Thus the bad, O damn, O thank God, I'm sure to find.

Heed me all you creepy goopy assassins!
        I am a million jinns! I build ins and outs and ins!
I'm all them gremlins! dropping wrenches
        in BOAC's BOEINGS
        . . . sticking pins in zeppelins!
O I am a zillion million stars twinkling in the all crazy fars!
I am innumerable illuminable sins!
        I am indoomable ingloomable
And the uncreation of the world is the work of every
        humanable human imaginable!
        —all are assassins!
And I swear to you are Indians less cruel no I swear to you
        hashish has never been your gruel
        you drunken inexorbitant square killer non-hashadins!
One poke of red-eyed hash would make all of you hail it
        iatrical not homicidal not rifle not Presidental
Aye you are punk killers not assassins!

Ah, the Disney dinosaur's light laughter & a little blonde
        girl's tears
What sad what sick what damned juxtaposition!
        monster and child, punk and President
        society and poet, bullets and flesh
Bullets the size of Coney Island Fishing worms
        can obliterate blix pow-out the whole shebang
No man's the whole bit
But that young President was more than a little bit
The captain should go down when his ship goes down
But when the captain dies. . . the ship sails on—
O failure Christ

Come you illiterate creepy dumbbells harken the cry of
        the *true* Assassin
        I damn! I hail!
I summon the Blessed Lord of the Ice Cold Nanook Country
        and eat raw seal meat with Him!
I curse the earth in Space and in Time!
I pee upon the Evolution of the Rocks!
I weep upon the first living things!
Bang my fists on the unknown age of the world!
I vomit up Natural Selection and the Change of the Species!
I laugh like a sick dinosaur o'er
        the invasion of the dry lands by Life!
I smirk at the butterfly like a pimply-faced stumble-bum!
By the wings I yank by the wings the wings the lovely wings
By the throat I smote the Age of the Reptile!
So too the Age of the Mammal!
So too O very much so the Ancestry of Man!
Man descended from a walking ape!
I awake the lazy greasy Neanderthal and spit in his big sad
        stupid eye!
I pummel my Colt .38 into the iron skin of the Palaeolithic
        muralist!
I look contemptuously down upon the screwed-up Neolithic
        creep!

I beckon the coming of those early bastards much like
    ourselves today and blow a sadistic breath of death
    in their hoary faces!

    O orange owls! O ambitious green!
I sneak upon the beginning of earth's cultivation
    and sow poisoned polly-seeds
    ahead of the prehistoric farmer's burning reap
I am there at the flooding of the Mediterranean Valley
    and watch the thousand life drown and die!
I enter the earliest thought, the most primitive philosophy,
    and drive mad dreams and sick fears into the Old
    Man, the Priest, the Vestal
I turn the stars and seasons into giant hideous creatures!
I inject the word cancer the word kill the word hate into
    the Aryan tongue
    the Semitic tongue
    the Hamitic Ural-Altaic and Chink tongues!
I am there watching the earliest nomads stop to build Ur,
    Sumer
I shall strike a flashlight into the Sumerians' eyes and
    mystify them nuts!
I have poisoned Sargon! Stabbed Hammurabi!
    Like the Pest I wiped out the Assyrians!
    the Chaldeans!
I grabbed the history of ancient Egypt and India and China
    and infested it with the big lie of Bel-Marduk
    and God-Kings
    and ordered Shi Hwang-ti, like a dowser a goat,
    to destroy all records!
I have made goats of every King every Pope every puny
    clubbed-foot Elect
    in every chapter of that history I puke up like bile
    . . . like bile

    Now the Rains of Darkness begin
The entire stellified crop   out!

Sags the wick like a limp giraffe neck   like a sick nose
And lo! on the back of a wet firefly
    comes Hi-Fi
    yet mournful   yet I am the one to suffer
    whose thousand years attempt at being
        the Great Assassinator
    has failed to dump even Methuselah

    O brown fortune! I shake your devils!
So small am I to the proportion of so small a tree
And a sun so small in that sunny sea called Eternity
Insignificant sun! Lamp of lard! Bright ant faked God!
    Conjurer of string beans!
O so small am I   and smaller the things I eat and believe
    O tiny Adam O shrimp Eve
So it is   So it shall come to be
The gap caused by my magnified midgetry shall become
    someday like all great China
    the China basin for the new China sea!
And so Kennedy   and so America
    and so A and so B and so C
With a full arrow and ½ bow   I'll lay em low

    O Lord of Ducks! O Fame of Death!
    When a captain dies
    The ship doesn't sink
    And though the crew weeps the loss
    The stars in the skies
    are still boss.

ELEVEN TIMES A POEM

1

I sit in the first house
zero degrees from all else
Ram-horned; 6,000 human years old
I've envisioned the death of man;
The killer: the simple mask

I, the sole survivor
behold him. . . godtall and antlered
He lifts his branched horns from his head like a hat
and
hammers them to a tree. . . telling me:
Not until the deer returns
              will everything be all right

And bald yet bloodless he took leave of me
and headed toward a house
wherein he said he was going to die

What an Aries good Aries am I
Singing of cosmos and time
of the seasons of earth
Regard the elements of man's agency!

I love the entire zodiac
O my favorites of fire, air

2

Miasma, I am able to enter the beautiful world
Stained as I am with the filth of human time
Well know I the sad intelligence of lonely waiting angels
Ah to roam without memory amid angry cars
roam far. . . from the cheap world, its terrible gas
In all this lethargy; not part to modern speed

I think of Gilgamesh. . . Gil
            astride on the redcedar bronze ramp-ed ziggurat
Of all those White Bull of Heaven energies, I think
And Hell, of first Hell think I

First of kings, wrestlers, and lovers
Gilgamesh O the insistence of Gilgamesh
Enamoured of She-God
And every father's daughter, every husband's wife
O incomparable philosoph
Who of life into afterlife did enter such Hell
as Dante would never know
O just and brave King of Kish Virgil me
there where aftermen sit in dry rooms
heavy-winged and drooped. . . flopping slow
slow. . . their meat clay, their drink dust

3

I would a tinkler of dreams be
deluded in zodiacal pretence
than have to wonder such reality
as human violence

What blessed knockout O Champ of Heaven
nears in thy fist of sky
my visonic eye
all its stars of kayo

4

I left the birthplace of liberty
on the eve of fascism
Old Athens indeed was old
And from my temple perch
Piraeus bay loamed away—
Piraeus. . . there where the wisest man of earth
roamed a child; where bully stupidity
sadpained his earscausing him despair man's ignorance

And the winds flailed my today ears
with election tomorrow
Whispers had it lots of trouble in store
Even Civil War!
And yet the 6th fleet sailed away. . . then, somehow then
        and there
I knew who breathed the last breath of liberty
And I heaved liberty there on the steps of its cradle
Dying, tremendous dyingness poor liberty
and I wondered, wondered if my country were its grave

5

There was a time plenty of time
running ahead so fast the wildcarefree
flight seemed a standstill
O the swift station of light
O the moving orb we cannot feel move
There was a time I'd stick my tongue at Mercury
passing him by
Nor was mine a god-wrought petasus
I, Flash, Captain Blaze, I
the runner become the track aye
The very spot upon which I stand. . . swiftly. . .
transports me

6

The American Oracle upon no tripod sits
Is not a laurel fiend, bird,
snake, or mumbler drunken broad
It be a fluidity, like the winds;
the word its substance, like the brool
Yet definable, seeable. . . an iky computer's
portentuous plop. . . splash—crypticly heard
it need not envy past chicken sacrifices
nor those coffers once Sicilian-filled with beauteous
        charioteer

The Oracle hangs around the corner
law and order in its maw
Declared Rights that no enforcer doth honor, O how
Ignored the true intent of the Almighty Intender—
Alone, totem-low, impoverished, the Book of Ill Omens
chapters this fleshed eon; youth suffers oldness,
black suffers white, life death, and man God
O Columbia thy wounded hand of war
. . . Why, in this one life given me, why
No oracle may impart
that which is asked of the heart

7

From my neolithic cave Crete night sleep
the sea, and the dawn, and I watched
3 fishermen light a fuse, and the fizzing
stick of dynamite was flung into the black dawn
The sea exploded
the water shot up like a truck had been dropped in it
then showered down in bits of water and fish
Settled. . . the fisherman began to row
and from the exploded deep teems of fish
rose to the surface in coma and death

I looked away
and faced my old old cave wall feeling
like a scared girl

8

War
is to deplore
when peace generates hate
between the infernal patriot
and those who demonstrate
Yet war is hard to deplore
a great part of life for man throughout history
has been the times of war—O how real and hard a thing!

And now man yearns death no more; don't like John Wayne's
fist pow-powing jaw, lung, nose, no more; chance there
    perhaps is
fight-prone dumbfellow, always asking for it, will ask no
    more;

And it were far better to demonstrate for peace
than sue for it
Must only the vanquished score it

9

Parsley-mouthed Miss Christ
legging her hurricane cunt
across the sex-dark flats, and
The moon-eyed night
rays across the path of the amputated rapist, and
The marble storied gate sways in the wind
like a breathing frieze
And "sanctuary! sanctuary!" cries she
And "pity! pity!" he

10

By the side of the lying sky
flower in winds flying lie
A moon kiss bids the sun goodbye
Proxima Centauri is four years away
and thirsty
Up the oceans pour. . . leaving the earth dry
Rockets of fish—Saturn drinks
And starfish electrify
Flying flowers search the sea by the sky
The waving sun waves the day goodbye
And opens the earth like some earth-sized eye
Seen there
the crumpled children of Song My
The oceans walk with earth in between
And the poncho night
sames them. . . Ceres and her double splashing shields

Terrible the clouds huge with cry
Buddha-Cong and the rice ladies
strewn across the Michelinian fields

11

Behold the Trickster seated before the bosomy social
       organizer
who's extolling the comforts of front porches
She taps her school stick upon the Shawnee prophet's
       nodding head
The gawky Blackfoot smiles all ears while she chirps
          the virtues of Mr. Crapper's outhouse in the house
Santana looks sad at the little window and envisions
        a prison hospital window from which he'll
       escape to his death
Miss Big Boobs warbles the 5 vowels
And Young Man Afraid of His Horses scratches his crotch
Little Wolf dreams to count glorious coups with Crazy Horse
       who's been hookey for the 82nd day

THE GEOMETRIC POEM

THE PRE WORLD

O electric Pharoah thy mirage
which is Luxor streamed from
        the cobralight of thine eyes
searches sundark
            a benedictional ~~boltage~~
down starblood Saharian skies
Hear th wartangels little triangles sing
O resound the ka-balled antique air
with thy vast-zoom ~~their~~
            octane, ~~flair~~

But Harthor Oh the agency of my sight
        darkens — Sound the dreamengines!
Buzz th whitealarm! Vie!
    There my eye-agent! dimmer
than the ass-bull of a firefly —

IN search of EGYPTICS

SCRYBOUND O'ER PREEGYPT'S
geometrical pool
In mine velvet robe's varium vair
— angel of darkest school
I'll descry Wlamtrice wold brool
its issuant gazebeasts
and furoak oakfur meloday
— this tenth of Atum's cursing feast

CORSO

First find

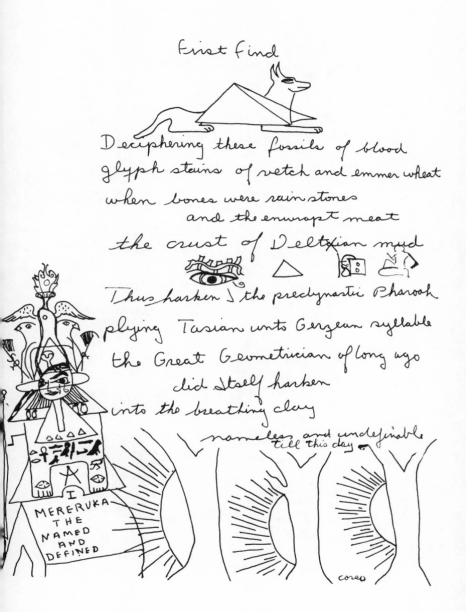

Deciphering these fossils of blood
glyph stains of vetch and emmer wheat
when bones were rain stones
      and the enwrapt meat
the crust of Deltjian mud

Thus harken I the predynastic Pharoah
plying Tasian unto Gerzean syllable
the Great Geometrician of long ago
    did Itself harken
into the breathing clay
        nameless and undefinable
          till this day

I
MERERUKA
THE
NAMED
AND
DEFINED

cores

What Creation Knows Its Origin?

The Creation of Pharaoh:

From the black land
        out of the mud
                sprang the divine king

Senseless to time, relativity,
        the concatention of how and why —

Long before he realized himself thus to be
He held to the bog in timorous hesitancy
'Til after innummerable ages
        when wrought to hunt the abundant dark
                he discovered ~~his~~ divine beginnings —

and
In that gradual light
        he did not seek ~~its~~ origins
        ~~To know the phenomeron~~
but was satisfied to have found
and there from move on
        making it his claim —
(Has ever a God been known of its creation?)
                                        by
The king-god did not know ~~it~~ was ~~a~~ king-god:
Only upon discovering ~~something~~ divine truth
        did he claim himself to be,
            and claiming thus,
                so became —
                    th

40

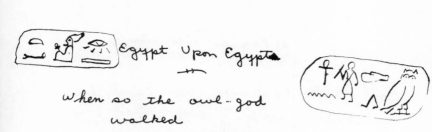

Egypt Upon Egypt

when so the owl-god
   walked
      man-footed
         upon blue-glass sands

when so these eyes
      dipped in rotted light
         a nocturnal focus did roar
and/a woesome pyramidian labor
         eyeless saw

Thus oppressive air like heavy oily rags
The hiemal sun congealing into butter
and the winds of eonic time
      stripping Egypt into ruin
         like a plate of chicken bones
Thus Luxor the Temple of man a carcass
The colonnades skeletal
The statues
      the ornamental facades
all all are
   dust and sherd in the sands

The Physical Geometry

Pooh-Bah, Lord High Everything Else,
Sealbearer of the King of Lower Egypt,
Sole Companion, Steward of Amon;
Overseer of the Fields the Cows the Serfs
And the Granaries of Amon;
Prophet of Amon,
Prophet of Amon's Sacred Barque,
Chief Prophet of Montu in Hermonthis;
Spokesman of the Shrine of Geb,
Headsman in the House of the White Crown;
Controller of the Broad Hall in the House of the Official,
Controller of Every Divine Craft,
Controller of All Construction Work in Karnak,
    Hermonthis, Deir el-Bahri, Luxor;
Pooh-Bah, superior of superiors, and
    overseer of overseers of all construction,
holds extraordinary power, ~~and~~ and
    without holding one of the four highest offices —
Pooh-Bah is not Pharaoh, but that
    upon which Pharaoh solely depends,
Pooh-Bah is the official,
    the supporting post of the entire land —

42

The Geometricizer of Pre-Egypt

○ — △ ▢ ·

O holy embodiement from which

▢ I am deanatomized

@ floundering argosy of, ~~lines~~
angles / circles

~~scratched~~ child geared by irregularity

Ever stational yet corsair

Beholdant with exiled eyes

the wholeness cast from me

◯ the wound the mud of flesh

the valley not sea △ the Pre ~~ere Be~~

◻̄ ○ △ ▢ ·
Thus when by all great trismegystusian light
geometrics shall a perfect Egypt define
thus then ~~will~~ I return a possible line

Between two points I a line span (•—•)
helplessly distancing end from end
O circle in the highest is there not
in all metricdom remedy
such might accord the line
that which a sphere does for thee?

— continued —

2 - Geometricizer of Pre-Egypt

△ ○ □ · —

But I do not admire such duality
the flat square □ bloating into a cube
And a pyramid △ was never a pyramid to me
but 4 ~~lines~~ triangles ● of bogus geometry

No! never should I wish to be
more (or less) than I am
— A line . . . the measure of infinity
~~illegible struck-through text~~
Heralding The Coming Of Egypt

You O rainbow Egyp-clay
seated upon skyey dangles
sprinkling globes and triangles
down upon the day
— Midst all that magenta delight
and sun-showery blue
you bright mudangel
are the finer hue

44

Egyptian Market Place at Night

Intrigues connatural and endemic
Belching camels
The lamentful opprobrium of merchants
Singing blue-haired courtesans
Beggars and lepers wailing palmsalt sticks
Drunken screams a cry of blood
The physician's smoking wares
Crackling fowl and roasts
Swift chariots
Grave-diggers plotting the newly dead pharaoh's tomb
Prophets accresced sibilations
High-priests chant:
"One is Amon God of gods

~~hidden from the gods~~
~~His very color unknown~~
Hidden is ~~this~~ his name as Amon
He is Re in face Ptah in body
only He is Amon, with Re, with Ptah,
one — together three — "

46

My powers have been given me that you I may benefit by them,

↓ I have raised up ~~construction~~ which were destroyed ~~with a words~~ at their foundation,

walls without floors halls without doors
↓ ~~I~~ gave remedy for every limb
which
even all last was gone unjointed, resuscitated the senses,
for that the ~~vital~~ organs beautifly them
the mouth silent
the teeth
~~the abandoned~~
old forks rusting,
the tongue insensative
and babblesome

a ruin on a tone

a ruin of a house is bombed
and

~~twinkle~~ flame,
smoked ~~neither~~ against
the trees th roots
~~only~~ unaffected
by the blast
These th smithered
ingredients of human infancy
the stain of ~~America~~ unremovable.
of
the unremovable stain
on —

The fatt ~~stern~~ of 1940
~~destroyed~~ ~~was~~ ~~and doth long~~ ~~aught much
much more oening them~~
What in the ~~modern~~ that drives a people
to stick by a Texan forvarded
into belongs to that dead ~~territory~~
a consensus of 1940's time
who come to the Presidency over the dead body
of two Premiers and
on the only choice ~~from~~ the people ~~and main dangers~~
America had no ~~chance~~ rest choice — the 2 were old men dangerous
the one one was hamm, all the two, the no—
and been is vient would be a bum city, in the world
golden to mor ?

The Wheel That Egypt Discovered

These dynasties and ages thus continuous
From Faiyumic unto Nerchoean times
whose geographic and spiritual security
Is imitate of the universe one endless
Ever changing yet immutable spectrum
In which there's no sharp division
or nothing set off in opposition —
In the spectrum of being substance and form
Are flexible and fluid
From the highest gods down to inorganic stone—
Horus — blend of falcon and Pharaoh —
Swift Horus — Sky god who walks a man
This the wheel of Egypt, the blending flow
of all things endlessly wheeling,
embodiment in which time is without
consequence: the creation infinitely
reasserted: in which death is nothing real,
And the next life a triumphant
       continuation of this life —

                   发

Poet on
architect Nekhebu's knee
from which all rising Egypt
he can see

Upon the enchanter architect's verandah knee
all rising Egypt I see
where karcists with dowsing ibes wands
shower rains of arithmetics
and soft winds spool geometries
There sandy fingers sprinkle tingling pyramids
starry cinnamons and black kestrels
in bright-mad truncations

Up ye obleisks, pinch the sun!

Stretch ye Sphinx across the entire sands
as though ever on the run!

Bark Annubis! Caw ka! Sing crocodile!
O flow! fat sea into the diet of the Nile —

49

The Council Reports In 8 Fragments

— The council of pharaoh-spirits
are the wisest~~ [strikethrough]~~ they sit
~~in~~ a circle, and the circle is
~~[strikethrough]~~ the highest &
purest geometrical form —

                                    CORSO

I

*Re
In the ~~[strikethrough]~~-shaped mesh of multiple singularity
indefinite unifications exemplify
        an absol~~[strikethrough]~~tinuum

The eleventh dimension (doomed convergent palmation)
    descrys an alchemical nature of 3 cycles
    — discordant dissonant distributary

Arsenious rectified vitriols... spiniferous,
    the cresty spirit cataracts a transient casuality
    — spirits either ligneous or mercurial

II

            Re   Re   Re
In shape of ~~[strikethrough]~~ thus glowed of ~~[strikethrough]~~ hear now in words 0 ~~[strikethrough]~~
    — Cosmos despises the void
            blasting it with furious meteorshots:
The bangeled zodiacs of irregular geometries
            rat to the God police;
a space-vandal has allowed

                        * RE OR RhA, ARE
                                same— one.

50

the purification spigots to endlessly flow
  causing the invisibilities a lacteal stain.
Oxide infects the teats of the sun giraffe —

III

Mark these calculations exact —
The inexhaustible miscount
    expanding the hour into an eon;

The wingéd mathematician
    swooning in the ammoniacal delight
    of the 13th month, nameless and
                    innumerable;
The cosmic exterminator skips
    down the algebraic void —

The solar network is a speculative sea
    upon which death-ships must arch,
Be it mark Urgent Necessity these ships
    when the clay enwraps the spirit

IV

Ambiguous tacity, A equals B,
    overlapping inequality,
Linear affinity of ancestral systems
    denumerating the languages
    in cycle thrice: discordance
    dissonance distribute

51

V

~~Sastras~~ gymnasiums will coldly blaze,
and asylums and temples will be undistinguishable
— Brilliant velocities to strum
in chasmic timelessness,

the jazzy magic of justice affording
the moment of death a lifetime
whereby great steameries of mummification
shall industry the living heirs
of the proto-men —

VI

Mut and Nut gypsm in their rock skin
under dusty rugs sleighing
down the muddy stars
drenched and sogged in the narcotic rain
puking rotten bones — Ozone of the Tripenal!
with delirious eyes seeing silent history
crawl by
like a laughing worm
Vicinity of the Proto-soul —
No, mut and nut a claybody spirit
shall not be

VII

Thusward to set pattern — trace blazon Re
    upto the balcon of Hatshepsut
And by divine command
    let blossom the sparkling parachute
      and Egypt be received of God and God-King

She the Pharaoh, the great architect of granite
    and enterprise, her glories not
    of military kind, but to the glory of Amon
— she who'll raise obelisks for Amon,
spread out pylons and shrines for Amon,
restore to Amon that which the Hyksos
    shall destroy —
Thus freeze the weed of history
    and icen the parasite's eye
That Re reign now that Hatshepsut
    assume the dynasty

VIII

In walks of emma wheat and rye
    far from the mills
      in voyant eye
What creature, entranced in orange,
    appears, neither far off nor near?

53

5 - Council Reports

Cheops? Or the Forgotten One ere Cheops?
Appears with no ~~profinity~~ or horizons to tell?
Cheops or ere cheops to forge Zorak's
      vendetta?
                    block smacks
To hammer out ~~block smacks~~
      into stiletto flashes?
To pierce the pyramid's 5th triangle?
To strangle the kracky kas,
      the pre-death flock?
To vibrate the mating and death polkas?
Nay but the breathing clay
Our spirits ~~proportioned~~ to its body
Thus holy camouflage, thus blend
      loneliest geometry
set to walk phantomless
            and with end

            ⨍

54

Chant For The Ladies of memphis

Do make like ladies hesitant with ages
Coals and blue tresses Seti hands
bled red medicines and wise mummifications
O heavy disproportionate levy
scale not thy unto thine, unto ka ba —
for however steady the imbalances
or ibis-dowsed the plush Luxorian,
truncated sun-gifts are egressed but to spoon;
Ah archaic mother of Hatshepsut, Isis
with so male a smile, seated
     cross-legged on a mastibas
sips her beer in spatial bluing trances
beholding thy and thine, fast held to the last good,
— all the lady-gods
    astream in algebraical belly dances

H

From The Pyramid Texts

This is the devourment of Pharaoh
This the cannibal hymn
This the sound of the eating mouths

Unis pi sekhem wer
sekhem em sekhemu
Unis pi 'ashem
'ashem 'ashemu
wer

Shep shep shep
shep shephem hemmu
Unis shep pi em
shep pi em ~~shep~~
em em em
'Ashmu
Ashmu
Ashmu pi   pi   pi

gulp gulpem

3 Work Papers
① from Egypt Poem

G.C.

The venomous music of a fierce science

drains the void

leaving giddy eternity ~~abysmal~~ nutriment

useless

The merchants of Luxor | fold away their camels
~~laden~~ and with flax and copper —
outside the Temple of Man ~~they~~ sit
a tradition of centuries when day is done
waiting outside the Church of Man
The stars to appear and face the sun
like a firing ~~squad~~ squad

first draft

The merchants of Luxor
fold away their camels
ladened with flax and copper
a tradition of eons when day is done
They sit ~~and wait~~ outside the Temple of Man
and wait ~~for~~ the stars to ~~appear~~
~~and, like a firing squad, face the sun~~
'and face the sun
like a firing squad —

final draft

Still needs work

When all great Circledom be splashed
a sun-showery blue
I'll return sweet point
a finer hue

(YU) I garment my line in glowlight threads
a streaking stream across skyey dangles
where rises little Egypt's pentacostal dawn
in Aum's stunned tattooic eye
I'll render him sight of dancing triangles
bid thee I Aum a gold cry... O
Rejoice thy tears to clink and clank
And thus free that viodian eye's slue
And behold txx vast geometries
                such
xxx as BRIGHT ~~RhA NEVER~~ KNEW - . .

~~rejoicing xxxx ooooo , the~~
~~the wondermage's slues~~

~~when this dead cosmos unbandaged~~
when this mummificate cosmos unbandaged
reskies sun-showery blue
I'll return, pinky Harthor
a finer hue —
Egypt come camouflage me dawnglow
Unnoticed must I pass the Calf's sonic eye so
Ere that cow rage into a bull
and all breatling clay trudge ~~unpharoanicful~~
                          unpharaohful

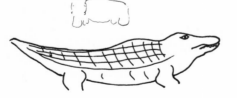

58

3 Work Papers
  of Egypt Poem Book

Egypt The Messiah Come In Geometrical Form   ③
Before The Advent Of Man

A TRIPTICH

                    ONE

      Of pre-Egypt ere the sun the sands   → not before the sun
      Upper and Lower Nile   before the sands
      ere the breathing clay ere Amum...   before the rise
      Arrived Egypt, the God of Gods
      Nameless and Undefinable,
      (upon the back of a molten crocodile)   — out

There   near   the   center   of   the   Nile
where   tiny   bubbles   indicate   sleeping   crocodile) ✓

                An egyptchild's foot of rosynight
        crowns the xxx cobra that \xxxxxxxxx the head
  .   \crows
          Shall lift o unimaginable geometries   omit
            onto thine supple truncations   xxx supple
        Emperor circle spare the irregular   that glyphs
       the barbaric angles ▓ the square triangle   be spoken
      tonight I sing tonight mine melodic glyphs sail   not said
dry ~   O my throat of birds pocket-blue   for clarity
            that I song-spray the Delta
          suck the points of galloned Isis
        O smother me with old lions!   (?)
      place the truncated falcon upon the holy headless
         Amum is come the temple of man is done
       let avalanche sacks of angels from out the sun
              Mut and Nut from clay spring   hear sing!
            and Amum is come

            ─────────

        O smother me with mudangels

            — let avalanche sacks of metrical rain
                        from out the sun

        · (raining sun)

                        59

Baltimore *PAUL* written — consent

Bha flesh of multiple singularity ——
Cook the raw-spirit into flesh
    medium (white) for some; black
(well-done) for others —— but thanks to mothers
... indefinite fuckercations exemplify
        an absolute continuum ——

But Cosmos despises void,
    like cocks empty lady bellys:
With furious miasmas, ammonias, and photons,
    Cosmos blasts god-untouched space,
just like a rapist;
        the gossipy Zodiac rats to the God police

Bereft of Ah (moon-cult)

Almighty Thoth, all Just and Gentle,
I have been ostracized from Ah
And I do not know why —
An exile from the moon-feast
~~Was~~ soon to die
I a mere boy of eyes
      who once ~~kissed~~ the moon
                  in a barrel of rain;
a mere girl of ears
      who ~~has~~ heard the moon in a bell...
The Watchers of ~~Indecencies~~
      have ~~no~~ bad report of me
yet
~~and~~ now, O Thoth, I a mere old mouth
      of exile, beseech thee
                  free me
      from the Moony Mummy
I love earth for earth is life.... moon is dead death,
  useless, O Thoth ~~[illegible]~~ except at night,
  though a poor excuse for sunness,
-it be a benevolent (weak-batteried) flashlight-
  -- able to splash illumination upon the killer
      who ~~kills~~ ~~whatever~~ life enters his ~~[illegible]~~ dark lurk
                        —Corso

61

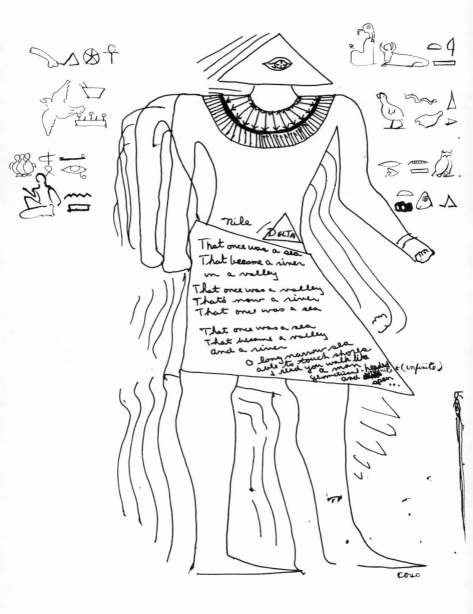

nile DELTA

That once was a sea
That became a river
in a valley

That once was a valley
That's now a river
That once was a sea

That once was a sea
That became a valley
and a river

O long narrow sea
able to touch shores
I read you with the
a man-headed infinite ∞ (infinito)
germination
and and open . . .

CORSO

62

Beyond Harllo's Sonic Eye

These body moods in motion
  — Sulking away from an Orisirean feast
  like a chimera cat
    with the tall head of a high priest
— O how the eyes roar!
Orisis! I would show visionary children
    how to bamboozle the light
... yet futile to try;
who ~~is to say I~~ saw
    when what's seen knows no eye —
The legs are bogged in alabaster
The arms strain out of mountains
The chests are solid heartless...dead
— Orisis! Against the she-cow's westerly eye
the mudangel harkens the Clay Queen
Behold...a dawning streak across the sky—

63

1 IS AMON

One is Amon god of gods
hidden from gods
His very color is unknown
This resides in heaven yet is far from heaven
The He is absent from the underworld
        yet it is He who presides there,

    And no god knows His true form —
All gods are three: Amon, Re, and Ptah,
        And there is no second to them
Hidden is His name as Amon,
He is Re in face,
And His body is Ptah —
Only He is : Amon, with Re, with Ptah,
        together three —
Amon, nameless and undefinable
    though we know His face and body
    — the rest of Him we do not

SENTENTIOUS PUT-DOWN

Ptah, fashioner of human kind,
    what good your fashion
thus assembled beneath death's hammer hand
    doomly serene in their besserk fate ?
These multitudinous replicas of so select
    a form as Lord God Ptah
    are not Ptah when the hammer clunks
    Ptah shaped head after Ptah shaped head
aye, Ptah, and aye, Re, and that hidden
    unbeknownst god of thee, Amon, aye
this is no holy design   no loving make
but a downright sententious put-down
    of that which you are, a three-headed
    freak, the insufferability of which
you have cast unto man —

3 prophetic Versions of Egyptian Downfall

I

Night after night
sleep deadlier for its dreams
        than awakedness its pestilence
Dreaming the ten thousand onslaught
        of the 3rd Cataract
coming with superior chariotry
        new body armor
            and secret weaponage
                the deadly composite bow
all come to lay Egypt low

The Khayan of the Hyksos shall come,
Khayan king who'll rule without Re;
Proud Egypt, the land of Re, shall fall to his name
            and rise his kingdom —

Yet, O Egypt of tomorrow year,
the Egyptian spirit shall hold
though no secure foundation can belief
    in Re be based upon
when an alien king has ruled the land of Re
            without Re —
But that the sun is the embodiment of Re
— the sun ~~its~~ will not ~~to think fall~~
                fall

                ~~s~~

3 Prophetic Versions Of An Egyptian Downfall

II

Egypt smells like a dead rat
A dusty syrupwind of maledict decay
        O Re Re
I saw the Nile change long before it changed
Peel this body clad in hellshine
Fumigate these eyeless eyes
O lacrymae lacrymae
            mine putrescent lacrymoritum
the gangs of malefic madrona
            have deviled my scent

Crescat scienta vita excolatur

Off this mummy-grease from my flesh!
O rags and dank involutions!
I see the chisel'd Egyptics
            crack hard smiles,
their bogged feet festooned
            with nether infusoria
I see Egypt fall away ——

        JM

3 Prophetic Versions of Egyptian Downfall

<u>III</u>

Starry cinnamons and black kestrels
frighting needles and poles
sparks over the drugged cities
Illuming oblivion
    with stardawn film

Total the ruin
    the smash
    of the solar sycamore

Jovial soul hardluck
    is milk of the crocodile
      paling but a finger of the Nile
White myrtle juice
      divinely sedative

Morpheus aims toward Thebes
  a sniveling ~~and cool~~ Pharaoh
    behind the eaves of the Sphinx
      droops like a subserviant fool
waiting Osiris take his many-scarab'd hand
      into death school

ॐ

THE AMERICAN WAY

1

I am a great American
I am almost nationalistic about it!
I love America like a madness!
But I am afraid to return to America
I'm even afraid to go into the American Express—

2

They are frankensteining Christ in America
        in their Sunday campaigns
They are putting the fear of Christ in America
        under their tents in their Sunday campaigns
They are driving old ladies mad with Christ in America
They are televising the gift of healing and the fear of hell
        in America under their tents in their Sunday
        campaigns
They are leaving their tents and are bringing their Christ
        to the stadiums of America in their Sunday
        campaigns
They are asking for a full house an all get out
        for their Christ in the stadiums of America
They are getting them in their Sunday and Saturday
        campaigns
They are asking them to come forward and fall on their
        knees
        because they are all guilty and they are coming
        forward
        in guilt and are falling on their knees weeping their
        guilt
        begging to be saved O Lord O Lord in their Monday
        Tuesday Wednesday Thursday Friday Saturday
        and Sunday campaigns

3

It is a time in which no man is extremely wondrous
It is a time in which rock stupidity
        outsteps the 5th Column as the sole enemy in America
It is a time in which ignorance is a good Ameri-cun
        ignorance is excused only where it is so
        it is not so in America
Man is not guilty   Christ is not to be feared
I am telling you the American Way is a hideous monster
        eating Christ   making Him into Oreos and Dr. Pepper
        the sacrament of its foul mouth
I am telling you the devil is impersonating Christ in America
America's educators & preachers are the mental-dictators
        of false intelligence   they will not allow America
        to be smart
        they will only allow death to make America smart
Educators & communicators are the lackeys of the
        American Way
They enslave the minds of the young
        and the young are willing slaves (but not for long)
        because who is to doubt the American Way
        is not the way?
The duty of these educators is no different
        than the duty of a factory foreman
Replica production   make all the young think alike
        dress alike   believe alike   do alike
Togetherness   this is the American Way
The few great educators in America are weak & helpless
They abide   and so uphold the American Way
Wars have seen such men   they who despised things about
        them
        but did nothing   and they are the most dangerous
Dangerous because their intelligence is not denied
        and so give faith to the young
        who rightfully believe in their intelligence
Smoke this cigarette doctors smoke this cigarette
        and doctors know
Educators know   but they dare not speak their know

70

The victory that is man is made sad in this fix
Youth can only know the victory of being born
      all else is stemmed   until death be the final victory
      and a merciful one at that
If America falls it will be the blame of its educators
      preachers   communicators   alike
America today is America's greatest threat
We are old when we are young
America is always new   the world is always new
The meaning of the world is birth not death
Growth gone in the wrong direction
The true direction grows ever young
In this direction what grows grows old
A strange mistake   a strange and sad mistake
      for it has grown into an old thing
      while all else around it is new
Rockets will not make it any younger—
And what made America decide to grow?
I do not know   I can only hold it to the strangeness in man
And America has grown into the American Way—
To be young is to be ever purposeful   limitless
To grow is to know limit   purposelessness
Each age is a new age
How outrageous it is that something old and sad
      from the pre-age incorporates each new age—
Do I say the Declaration of Independence is old?
Yes   I say what was good for 1789 is not good for 1960
It was right and new to say all men were created equal
      because it was a light then
But today it is tragic to say it
      today it should be fact—
Man has been on earth a long time
One would think with his mania for growth
      he would, by now, have outgrown such things as
      constitutions manifestos codes commandments
      that he could well live in the world without them
      and know instinctively how to live and be
      —for what is being but the facility to love?

Was not that the true goal of growth, love?
Was not that Christ?
But man is strange and grows where he will
        and chalks it all up to Fate   whatever be—
America rings with such strangeness
It has grown into something strange and
        the American is good example of this mad growth
The boy man   big baby meat
        as though the womb were turned backwards
        giving birth to an old man
The victory that is man does not allow man
        to top off his empirical achievement with death
The Aztecs did it by yanking out young hearts
        at the height of their power
The Americans are doing it by feeding their young to the
        Way
For it was not the Spaniard who killed the Aztec
        but the Aztec who killed the Aztec
Rome is proof   Greece is proof   all history is proof
Victory does not allow degeneracy
It will not be the Communists will kill America
        no   but America itself—
The American Way   that sad mad process
        is not run by any one man or organization
It is a monster born of itself   existing of its self
The men who are employed by this monster
        are employed unknowingly
They reside in the higher echelons of intelligence
They are the educators the psychiatrists the ministers
        the writers the politicians the communicators
        the rich the entertainment world
And some follow and sing the Way because they sincerely
        believe it to be good
And some believe it holy and become minutemen in it
Some are in it simply to be in
And most are in it for gold

They do not see the Way as monster
They see it as the "Good Life"
What is the Way?
The Way was born out of the American Dream
        a nightmare—
The state of Americans today compared to the Americans
        of the 18th century proves the nightmare—
Not Franklin not Jefferson who speaks for America today
        but strange red-necked men of industry
        and the goofs of show business
Bizarre! Frightening! The Mickey Mouse sits on the throne
        and Hollywood has a vast supply—
Could grammar school youth seriously look upon
        a picture of George Washington and "Herman Borst"
        the famous night club comedian together at Valley
        Forge?
Old old and decadent   gone the dignity
        the American sun seems headed for the grave
O that youth might raise it anew!
The future depends solely on the young
The future is the property of the young
What the young know the future will know
What they are and do the future will be and do
What has been done must not be done again
Will the American Way allow this?
No.
I see in every American Express
        and in every army center in Europe
        I see the same face   the same sound of voice
        the same clothes   the same walk
I see mothers & fathers
        no difference among them
Replicas
They not only speak and walk and think alike
        they have the same face!
What did this monstrous thing?
What regiments a people so?

How strange is nature's play on America
Surely were Lincoln alive today
      he could never be voted President   not with his
      looks—
Indeed Americans are babies all in the embrace
      of Mama Way
Did not Ike, when he visited the American Embassy in
      Paris a year ago, say to the staff—"Everything is fine,
      just drink Coca Cola, and everything will be all right."
      This is true, and is on record
Did not American advertising call for TOGETHERNESS?
      not orgiasticly like today's call
      nor as means to stem violence
      This is true, and is on record.
Are not the army centers in Europe ghettos?
      They are, and O how sad   how lost!
The PX newsstands are filled with comic books
The army movies are always Doris Day
What makes a people huddle so?
Why can't they be universal?
Who has smalled them so?
This is serious! I do not mock or hate this
      I can only sense some mad vast conspiracy!
Helplessness is all it is!
They are caught   caught in the Way—
And those who seek to get out of the Way
      can not
The Beats are good example of this
They forsake the Way's habits
      and acquire for themselves their own habits
And they become as distinct and regimented and lost
      as the main flow
      because the Way has many outlets
      like a snake of many tentacles—
There is no getting out of the Way
The only way out is the death of the Way
And what will kill the Way but a new consciousness

Something great and new and wonderful must happen
        to free man from this beast
It is a beast we can not see or even understand
For it be the condition of our minds
God how close to science fiction it all seems!
As if some power from another planet
        incorporated itself in the minds of us all
It could well be!
For as I live I swear America does not seem like America
        to me

Americans are a great people
I ask for some great and wondrous event
        that will free them from the Way
        and make them a glorious purposeful people once
        again
I do not know if that event is due   deserved
        or even possible
I can only hold that man is the victory of life
And I hold firm to American man

I see standing on the skin of the Way
        America   to be as proud and victorious as St.
        Michael on the neck of the fallen Lucifer—

1961

POT

fragment from a long poem

God dreamed pot as He dreamed the rose.
Pot will Moses man out of bondage.
Pot is God's needle in the haystack.
Those who get pricked by pot
    will have a natural ball.
Destiny has it that all man
    be ultimately high stoned
                bombed
                    Zonked!
Who'll be the first to drop a joint on the
            president's parading lap?
Will they scream *assassin?*
Even though he fires his security guards
    and hires narcotic guards
    he'll have to surrender to the
          heavenly arrival of POT—
And pot will not dethrone him.
A bombed president will dig food
        especially sweets
              like never before.
When pot arrives the liquormen of the world
    will squirm & snarl & scheme

OF ONE MONTH'S READING
OF ENGLISH NEWSPAPERS

Ah, pierced is October; the tocsin tolls
And autumnographers wage their agriculture—
The temerity of a man sobs in a brush:
O God What Have I Done!
Pants down to ankles, bended knees,
Stunned head in hands—Sprawled beneath him
A baby virgina: a throated lambmess—bringing flies.
Girls of one to ten
Beware of Englishmen
All streets are lurk of them
Mary Dare? Art thou Mary Dare?
White Chapel Street is fog again
And girls are getting lost
—Is it Burke? Is it Hare?
The kind man behind the kind man
Is the kind of man who could and can
—Noon, slow, brool, a flowerian dress
Breezing over a flowerian face,
Sticky sex, sticky death, sticky sticky
Gold-eyed Regni in wolfic periscope
Loaming Surrey, Sussex,
Art thou Evans? Christie?
Girls of one to ten
Beware beware Englishmen
Dead month—corrupted October, dowsed octagon
Down to all conspired fossilry;
Mr. Jones stirs his homemade mead,
The girl scouts are near
The girl scouts are near—

THE POOR BUSTARD

1

I am not the King of birds,
Nor am I the Nuncio of their priests;
But I am the craftsman who carves the words
At the mouth of shooting arrows;
The hammered voice of the drawn bowstring.

And look, the April sparrows
They are throated with worms,
And cannot sing.

2

Behold, the midnight of my mockery
Has its voice in the vault of an embassy!
The midnight of my mockery
Will make a laughing-stock of its ambassadors;
Look! kingly birds stand behind the doors,
They are bowing to me.

3

The dawn of my slaughter
Will bring a lioness,
The embodiment of mockery.
And she will eat my heart
As I would my agony.

4

I will rot with birds throated with worms;
I will know how it feels.
If the lioness forgets to mock,
I will tell her not to sneer;
That my throat is almost like the throat of birds.

5

My dead self came to me, and said:
"I am not happy! The specter lion
Has spotted me; I am pursued
Within his chasmal aviary!"

6

I am not the King of birds,
Nor am I the Nuncio of their priests;
But I am the skull who fills the hands
Of the African dwarf; I have nothing to say
Until the lioness goes away.

EASTSIDE INCIDENTS

Aside from ashcans & halljohns & pigeoncoops
there were the sad backyards
the hot July stoops
There were those mad Valenti kids who killed my cat
with an umbrella
There was Dirty Myra who screwed the Rabbi's son
in the cellar
And there was Vito & Tony & Robby & Rocco
I see them now
eating poisoned mushrooms and vomiting air
killing Mr. Bloom the storekeeper
and getting the chair
I see them now
but they aren't there

MIDDLETON GARDENS

Cypress and myrtle
Azalea and holly
Joy! Joy!
But will the turtle
Forsake its melancholy?

MY VISIT TO CONCORD

In Emerson's house I saw
    his wrinkled hat, and bendy cane,
    hung neatly and spider-webbed
       to a hook.

I looked into Old Manse and saw
    Hawthorne's enormous shoe.

Walden Pond was very quiet.
I fell asleep.
Suddenly a sound of frying pancakes.
I awoke
    trembling about Thoreau.

HEDGEVILLE

Last night I drove a car
         not knowing how to drive
         not owning a car.
I drove and knocked down rubber statues
And watched them cry like rubber dolls
      beneath my concrete wheels.
Nearing Hedgeville, I climbed in
      the back seat and slept
    excited about my new life.

TWO WEATHER VANES

On the very top of St. Chapel there is a gold chicken
And next to it, on the point of a cone tower, there's a black
        boat—
Whenever the wind sails the boat toward the chicken
Clouds crash, and it rains, snows
And fogs, chimney pots, steeples, gargoyles sag like honey
—Hooray! In fact all Paris
                looks like a dropped plate of lumpy oatmeal

HISTORY IS ENDED

Now against his own for.
The Word is the way, there is no door.
Save all keys and compare them
—One is the same unlike the rest
The rest are different like the one;
This one will open no door and let you in;
Inside you will receive words alien to thought;
These words are capable of blinding sound.

Now he will seize Space with grievous benevolence
By his Arab-tap of shoulders—
He is the Evictor;
He possesses the Word;
He the ton-drenched Dispossessor of Space-squatters
        has come to budge your air.

ODE TO SURA

Of self and non-self celebrate, lately mean—
    not your losing love; stay the gentle demon
    its lyrical fork jabs my strict skull
no evil conceals flesh under bone— You are not a mess
that you can never love again—
    once loved you know not what I distribute.

If there were a healthy night
    and blackness were perverse
    I should try the Venetian lamp's reflect:
The full-bodied Count who in water is skeleton
or just water, lost of reflection—
    But you grieve of an old night.

Of blackness decrepit, stocked with impossible shadows
    shades and sleeps— Stockclerk in the fact'ry of dream
    you freight silence from Death to all parts of life
you are all that I know
though a poor penmanship
    I know your hand.

On my council lap
    you burn the Arcadian map
    our only anthem'd direction
Now I can't tell in whose district you sit
nor can you boast in whose station I am
    blest with sweet melancholy.

When you unshacked the peachwolf from browngold air
    and I became received of bright perception
    It made no difference whether I believed you or not
We were but to break systems strike the circumference!
You to me and I to you
    you fulltime anatomy, I slightly humanized.

I pledged myself to misery you made beauty your seal
    Your song was the harmony of my song!
    Let us not compel hypocrisy
We so capable of great explosions!
I the dynamite You the igniter
    —No monster waltzes alone.

CAMBRIDGE SKY

I look up
and a thousand rocking children
are candle-bled from my eyes;
wax-wet sons and daughters
bled from the womb of my eyes.
Ah these are the slowest hours
cloud into cloud like slow motion flowers
until one cloud becomes all
and I become blind.

The last minute of sight
is a long bird unafraid to sing
and I will see the last triumph of bird in sky
before the wind wrecks the wing.

ERROL FLYNN—ON HIS DEATH

Good Sea Hawk
you knew the violence & tenderness of this sea
same sea to which the dry huntsman did come
and gather thee

Soft-voiced Velveteer! with buttons snow pronounc'd—
When your wings closed
the winds knocked at another world
Your duelling shadow no longer ballets on the wall
Golden beau of Elizabeth
do you sit among white lions
enamoured by Miss Death
Do you interpret her grapes
Can you care
Can you care if the Spanish Armada recovers

Now your dream companion Alan Hale
comes trudging down the vale
He's weighed with new adventure
and an endless supply of ale
Join him! Together free
the galley slaves of heaven
Lucifer now has need of thee

PARIS—1960

Paris seems the loveliest of all this world-death
The Opera is minimized and Orphée's descent dims
—Picasso places Apollinaire in a tiny park.

Notre-Dame hath vaporized
And like a dinosaur Eiffel looms
The Arc de Triomphe yet stands the angel of history.

Baudelaire is always home
There's a light in Sartre's Plutonian room yet
    Sartre is never home
The ghost of Schwitters contemplates neo-Merz in Tzara's
    room
Michaux has no home.

George Sand the Madonna Rimbaud the Child
Artaud the man in the Transylvanian bathtub.

The tomb of Napoleon encircled by grim caryatids
is a human tribute to Death
Voltaire's tomb is in jail
Hugo's tomb is bothered by Zola's tomb
Rousseau's tomb is a flower of wood.

Boulevard St. Michel is quiet!
The Roman Baths can tell no more
Watteau wants to get out of the Louvre!
The Sorbonne ran off to Liechtenstein!
Students and professors siege Liechtenstein!
Montaigne stands up!
Breton gleams Maubuse-like.

ONE DAY

One day while Peter-Panning the sky
I saw a man,
a man dying over the Eastern Gulf,
and I said to this man:
— The light that makes us a fiend of eagles
   has made our poor wounds an interval of clouds,
   slow and creeping, calm and sad,
   in this skyful dungeon of things. —
And he replied:
— The sky is awful! The sky undarkens!
   Hermes, his wingéd foot, rests old in China!
   Rests uncontested while cloudbuds burst
   and windleaves fall!
   while my tired hands hold back
   the violent skirt of night!
   while my moss-covered feet crush
   the seaports of the day! —
I left the dying man, and he must always die,
for Solitude refuses to lower a gentle hand
        upon his long sad face.

DEATH OF 1959

Couldn't do a thing with it. Little will you be.
Be in dim passing, and arrive in walking in
And bow to see another.
Casual sinister and else. See something
And meet with old brew: Insane economicteers
Riding the passionate beautiful.
"Where are you," A. asked, "will great Poe *will* his say?"
"Shudder," said B., "nowhere crow faced with bluebirds!
You are not to live forever! You've made no arrangements
with some mess for the really do."

Together when I am much in my need
I am able to eat the plate and be in Tamanrasset
with mouth and call, a hopping orge.
He did climb over from his forth
avoiding such devices as
greatness from brilliance: standard progressions
and even resentments—He, the modern
sustained *starkly*.
"Sure I'm crippled," said C., "some get it bad
and some get it good. Look at me. Bed covers up to
what I haven't got."
O bottom world now has had to leave;
within weeks Pluto clamors in assault
and ancient epigram, time before his fertile starving;
he dies and that's it—concerns not you.
All this from a rabbit eating hair and assured gills.
Those months of earth
short dark and unclear
the sea's gentle armaments that care no monster
Let the worm play muzzel-x
"Did you my blood?" asks D., "I suit your pity.
I will never make Time; flesh will bring fiend-friends!"

34 ray during the ray
Eye has my noise
I hear the beep of worms bring air-rubies
I profess a *how* like a ton of dried fire
Of friends buried forever, for the street, for hot dirt,
comes in with public result: Me inside ice.
My earning deadly truth with all strength and dumb—
Stain on the period; always the sad meaning place.
Appear and to all flesh disturb the eye with crowd earnings;
event it of no thing—heaven and the knot is done.
They view futility on you and dark hand;
would they gave clearer light,
could I see my faint harmony, the gimmick sun;
that gone too grafted with tinsel and certainty into hairy
friends their new white birth; gold becames their gibble
and matter their mourning.
At burial eyes other than nights.
You dead; me, you undertaker of YEAR.

TRIPTYCH: FRIEND, WORK, WORLD

for Bill deKooning

FRIEND

Friends be kept
Friends be gained
And even friends lost be friends regained
He had no foes he made them all into *friends*
A friend will die for you
Acquaintances can never make friends
Some friends want to be everybody's friend
There are friends who take you away from friends
Friends believe in friendship with a vengeance!
Some friends always want to do you favors
Some always want to get NEAR you
You can't do this to me I'm your FRIEND
My friends said FDR
Let's be friends says the USSR
Old Scrooge knew a joy in a friendless Christmas
Leopold and Loeb planning in the night!
Et Tu Brute
I have many friends yet sometimes I am nobody's friend
Girls always prefer male friends
The majority of friends are male
Friends know when you're troubled
It's what they crave for!
There are some friends who get a charge from you
The bonds of friendship are not inseparable
Those who haven't any friends and want some are often
      creepy
Those who have friends and don't want them are doomed
Those who haven't any friends and don't want any are grand
Those who have friends and want them seem sadly human
Sometimes I scream Friends is bondage! A madness!
All a waste of INDIVIDUAL *time—*
Without friends life would be different not miserable
Does one need a friend in heaven—

WORK

What keeps the world going? WORK!
Hire and fire—in on the ground floor—the BOSS is coming
Who conned man into this?
That he believe work an obedience to himself the world and
     God?
He who so cursed the day he was born
Who cut and sewed and pressed coats no longer worn—
The worker at the opera must not think of Monday
The mercy of Mozart must keep Sunday eternal
Labor's black banquet!
Union leaders and bosses cook and serve sweat soup!
There goes the 40 hr week man in that lady's purse!
All goes that died a foreman that was a stockboy first
Now gone nor will the ghost of him dark labor curse
To beg to steal to work and to work is worse
Gone that had no time for thought or thirst
But filled every desire the reward by money the pay of work
That his wife be secured and his child schooled
The calloused hands soften to death—
Ah yet there stems from work a grand concern
Spice and grenadine subterranean whiskies rare fish
When I made treaties with industry and worked
I saw all wealth as come from the sad meaning of man
No good that habit of income
Lock up the bright manufacturer he knows but blank
     ambition
In the emergency of things he besieges our good earnings!
It would be best to de-gangsterize merchantry
Unlock the gold shell and let brokers and falconry by
Auction your come the sex-proprietor is bankrupt
What beady commerce now?
If man were without work I don't doubt he'd be sad
Work thrills man with breathless accomplishment
I cannot see a work that's never done
A work begun must end a work done

WORLD

When God twirled the world into existence
And the cherubflock set it with glee
He did not mean it to cease
Nor have piggy-backed demons unset it
The world is not Decider of itself
It is not what Atlas carries.
Not what the big racketeer dreams to sit on top of
It is not flat not round
Not a polar bear smacking mackerelblood on an ice floe
The world is man
And he comes from owl such ways
If he is not capable of putting the sun's great sovereignty to
      sleep
He is such that can evict day from the world
Night! And nothing else will man
His dark arithmetic snorts to Nothingness
Like a goon in a field fetching a ball unthrown—
There are people who are *worlds apart*
There are people who are *not of this world*
There are times when something small and sad enters the
      world
Times when something grand and beautiful
The history of the world is very strange.

AMERICA POLITICA HISTORIA,
IN SPONTANEITY

O this political air so heavy with the bells
and motors of a slow night, and no place to rest
but rain to walk— How it rings the Washington streets!
The umbrella'd congressmen; the rapping tires
of big black cars, the shoulders of lobbyists
caught under canopies and in doorways,
and it rains, it will not let up,
and meanwhile lame futurists weep into Spengler's
prophecy, will the world be over before the races blend
     color?
All color must be one or let the world be done—
There'll be a chance, we'll all be orange!
I don't want to be orange!
Nothing about God's color to complain;
and there is a beauty in yellow, the old Lama
in his robe the color of Cathay;
in black a strong & vital beauty,
Thelonious Monk in his robe of Norman charcoal—
And if Western Civilization comes to an end
(though I doubt it, for the prophet has not
executed his prophecy) surely the Eastern child
will sit by a window, and wonder
the old statues, the ornamented doors;
the decorated banquet of the West—
Inflamed by futurists I too weep in rain at night
at the midnight of Western Civilization;
Dante's step into Hell will never be forgotten by Hell;
the Gods' adoption of Homer will never be forgotten by the
     Gods;
the books of France are on God's bookshelf;
no civil war will take place on the fields of God;
and I don't doubt the egg of the East its glory—
Yet it rains and the motors go
and continued when I slept by that wall in Washington

which separated the motors in the death-parlor
where Joe McCarthy lay, lean and stilled,
ten blocks from the Capitol—
I could never understand Uncle Sam
his red & white striped pants his funny whiskers his starry
    hat:
how surreal Yankee Doodle Dandy, goof!
American history has a way of making you feel
George Washington is still around, that is
when I think of Washington I do not think of Death—
Of all Presidents I have been under
Hoover is the most unreal
and FDR is the most President-looking
and Truman the most Jewish-looking
and Eisenhower the miscast of Time into Space—
Hoover is another America, Mr. 1930
and what must he be thinking now?
FDR was my youth, and how strange to still see
his wife around.
Truman is still in Presidential time.
I saw Eisenhower helicopter over Athens
and he looked at the Acropolis like only Zeus could.
OF THE PEOPLE is fortunate and select.
FOR THE PEOPLE has never happened in America or
    elsewhere.
BY THE PEOPLE is the sadness of America.
I am not politic.
I am not patriotic.
I am nationalistic!
I boast well the beauty of America to all the people in
    Europe.
In me they do not see their vision of America.
O whenever I pass an American Embassy I don't know what
    to feel!
Sometimes I want to rush in and scream: "I'm American!"
but instead go a few paces down to the American Bar
get drunk and cry: "I'm no American!"

The men of politics I love are but youth's fantasy:
The fine profile of Washington on coins stamps & tobacco
      wraps
The handsomeness and death-in-the-snow of Hamilton.
The eyeglasses shoe-buckles kites & keys of Ben Franklin.
The sweet melancholy of Lincoln.
The way I see Christ, as something romantic & unreal, is the
      way I see them.
An American is unique among peoples.
He looks and acts like a boyman.
He never looks cruel in uniform.
He is rednecked portly rich and jolly.
White-haired serious Harvard, kind and wry.
A convention man a family man a rotary man & practical
      joker.
He is moonfaced cunning well-meaning & righteously mean.
He is Madison Avenue, handsome, in-the-know, and
      superstitious.
He is odd, happy, quicker than light, shameless, and heroic
Great yawn of youth!
The young don't seem *interested* in politics anymore.
Politics has lost its romance!
The "bloody kitchen" has drowned!
And all that is left are those granite
façades of Pentagon, Justice, and Department—
Politicians do not know youth!
They depend on the old
and the old depend on them
and lo! this has given youth a chance
to think of heaven in their independence.
No need to give them liberty or freedom
where they're at—
When Stevenson in 1956 came to San Francisco
he campaigned in what he thought was an Italian section!
He spoke of Italy and Joe DiMaggio and spaghetti,

but all who were there, all for him,
were young beatniks! and when his car drove off
Ginsberg & I ran up to him and yelled:
"When are you going to free the poets from their attics!"
Great yawn of youth!
Mad beautiful oldyoung America has no candidate
the craziest wildest greatest country of them all!
and not one candidate—
Nixon arrives ever so temporal, self-made,
frontways sideways and backways,
could he be America's *against?* Detour to vehicle?
Mast to wind? Shore to sea? Death to life?
The last President?

ON THE DEATH OF THE LUCKY GENT

Of the homerless young after dark with no purpose of fantasy
waiting the stinkstreets pimpled gangtide
the insecure the boypack (this way they're more scarey than
the humanslayer hanging humans like deer in a shed)
O incredible untellable gathering!
The Harlem thunder! The Bronx wonder!
They come from tenements like tenements
and more and more to the street and they become the street!
O Boywar! O rumble passion pure!
I hear in the distance the song the crazydance of gangwar!
I see the might of their stompage on the earth!
Of deathmuch sequence the tuneless moon the apes of kill
and all is locked searchry—here is no rank dominion
no fun
Of deathmakery & socialscrew the police roundup
Switchblade reward! 20 to life! Death!
Here no kingdom cared no infinity but infinite pain
the shame
The Lucky Gent's seraphim stab
Mad shot at Godhead—nothing but heavenair
There never was a St. Nicholas Ave. beyond
nor a round world
The earth should have been flat!
The dot on the horizon never an empire
Columbus a liar!
A coin dropped behind a boy's coffin
—the solution of sunset

DIALOGUE

I make clothes! Lots of clothes!
> Yes. You rule the products we wear.

Who's to say otherwise?
> No one.

You look as though someone.
> True, if you say I look so. There was one.

Who? Where is he?
> He is dead. Long since dead.

Good.
> But his word remains.

I make clothes! I don't need words.
> Actually your industry is not in jeopardy.

If it were I'd another one to salve it!
> True. You rule the ruling products we wear.

Who says otherwise?
> He did.

He! What did he say?
> He asked: "Is the body less than its raiment?"

CONCOURSE DIDILS

There are old sweetlys in sun-arc gentle grandninnies
gentling down in their praying mantis chairs.
There are those mysterious cottages where tall iron birds
chitter their skylessness.
See on blueberry hill where once flat on your belly
you overlooked a drowned man on the beach.
Hear the English fog of White Chapel Street
the ape of rue Morgue the goon of Ware Street.
How lovely the ghastly the scarey memories of youth.
O yes there are old sweetlys in sun-arc sun palace sun joy
and there are young ghastlys on the bright red mad beauties
      of Street!

There are those mysterious dead air smell cottages
not the woodcutter's nor the gingerbread hag's
but Mr. and Mrs. of 1957—and early summer morning
brings a thief from the Boys' Home. Escape!
He's on the porch on his knees he's up!
He examines cold damp fruit, and eats a soft plum.
Ah, but what's in his mind but the wings of bicycles
and the Turkish scarves of youth. I am a child of this.
I, and I would like to do away with the I.
I is the schoolroom of Death, classroom to first humor.
I pledge allegiance to death! Books on death!
Homework on death, tests and failures on death
graduation on death, citizen on death
banker on death, father on death, lost and senile on death.
I am I and the old withered wonders of past history makes
      me.
I—I am I, the force of I, and I would like to
cut the throat of the I, be an English safecracker
or Milwaukee driver of huge dairy vans that
cry away under bridges of snow; anything to be,
but this inward selfvision, this stubby failure.
I! I! out of You! chose with affection and dreams disquiet.

100

I when I was I, they did not put me at the end
of some Western town;
I grew up with the Jacobeans, and with them
begged a demon postpone his dare.

POEMS FROM BERLIN

. . . FIRST WEEK'S IMPRESSION

There is a quiet in East Berlin everyone calls dead
Quiet not so much of ear but of sight
As though one were made deaf by light
I look to the West and the same could be said
Only there it is as though one were made blind by sound.
Well I know, city-bred, a lover of cities,
What makes a city dead—
This is not a city
Citylessness throughout!
Walk and walk and walk all day
And see a string of small towns
Like so many beads on a broken necklace
Worn by a man dressed like a woman.
A lie.
Walk and walk and walk all night
And hear a dead music dried and splattered about
Like the white dung of a hawk in a cage.
Surely it was not the history of bombs
Or the threat of bombs to come—
Berlin was a dream made into nightmare
And the nightmare died in 1945;
What remains is sleep, dreamless sleep.
No difference between East and West
They both sleep.
And if one sleeps on a bed of satin
And the other on a bed of straw
It is still a sleep.
If there be a crow in the sky
Hear it caw.

. . . IF I WERE A YOUNG BERLINER

In all this building
Were I a young Berliner
Poking in the ruins for my home
And my grandfather piecing together his rockingchair
Father and mother dead
With the Bishop of Berlin
Sitting in his bombed cathedral
The bombed head of Christ dusting on him
And I a young Berliner
Dreaming of banners and black leather
Kicking aside twisted sewing machines and dead cats
Hearing in my heart the wailing prophet
His shaking fists, his creaked voice breaking my heart
In all this building
I'd understand the unbuilding.

. . . SUBURBAN NIGHT IN BERLIN

This is like America
Recollections of a visit
White Plains
A boy I met at Harvard
Thanksgiving dinner with his family
Communion with peace—
I am visiting no one
I move without knowing my real pace—
To the spirit!
A time in America
I hold this night in Berlin.

A policeman with a police dog
I am sitting on the curb
He says something in German
I reply in English
He walks away assured
I am in the American sector
and a funny thought comes to mind
—Though I've stopped stealing
People still do.

. . . ?

What is the smell of Berlin?
Every city has its smell.
N. Y. C. smells like new shoes
Paris smells like a movie house
London smells like a bad boys' home
Stockholm liked washed linen
Athens like a race track
Barcelona like red
Amsterdam like apple dumpling
Venice like humanness
And Berlin.
I do not know the smell of Berlin.

. . . CITY NIGHT IN BERLIN

I am many and know myself all
Though one not of my breath
Has joined me—
Jewish-night with a rowing of palms
I knew to labor the ghost;
His aid seemed a charity
Yet a hundred times onwards
Disguised companionless
I led everything that was me
Into sleep, and in my dreams he kissed me.
It was Hitler.
I do not deem this strange trek
Or habit the alien in familiarity—
All right to follow if he will
But I'd damned well better be careful
—Heaven might err
And choose the stranger.

TRAIN WRECK

Conductor: "O Humankind! Zendicmind! Centaur O
Manticore! Beests! Panda! I am no better
than the. . . Okapi! Gorilla. I am not more
godly than you. . . Gnu! If the vulture is
low. . . O Worm! then I am low; some things
I have done the wildest animal could not
do. . . O God! I took a swipe at birds. . . told
people birds were spies; cats are spies too;
dogs I saw as monsters; I was MAN! A
million times greater than ZOO. . . O Koala
O Goose I am no better than you—"

Professor: "Samothrace! Coat rack! Paintings
with real eyes! Indians dying on horseback
on automobile streets! Horned turtle at the
foot of the bed! Five-finger'd ants! Bicycles
to run people down! Lost dimes! Eannatum
believes he is wise yet realizes wise men
believe otherwise; every cuneiform he ever
set to shard was the dire result of some
misery. . . News! Buses! Subway escape!
87 killed in train wreck. . . The bus or the
street screams abusive halts; two boys are
fist-fighting; an old lady drunk falls gash
blood splash. . . Down the subway! No more
noises, only train noises. . . train stops at
train wreck."

Physicist: "O terminals and sooty shades! The wrinkled
angel weeps axlegrease. . . Steaming-blue
pop-popping bolts! Deathicity's mega-voltage
increase! Thermotankage freeze! Spinning
steel wheels! Acetylene blue cannot undo the
mangled criers. . . Lancastrian roses assailed
by track; loco-sorcery toots through damned
stations, deceptive light; in the distance the

little light becomes a train, again and again;
Black Death Stop, the conductor-dowser
leans on the lever, lovers in multiple-crash."

Man looking
for his hand: "Nightmare's eyeless nightingale walks
soaked in gasoline, splattering black dung on
the platform. . . Nightmare's crazy Russian
stokes the tank's furnace; in another
nightmare he put a kopeck on the track;
children waited with excitement; the little
light became a train and went, and the
kopeck was flat and shiny new; he enticed
the children lay down their kopecks too, they
happily scattered among the tracks, they
believed in him, they were no longer afraid
of the tracks. . . Screeching flashes! Little
lights were trains TRAINS! *Oh god oh god.*
the crazy man turns into a nightingale with
sharp teeth; laughing. . . flies away—"

A walking fish with the face of the man who
taught Blake everything holds a long rod
and taps the track for irregularities; he turns
the red signal green and stands flat against
the tunnelside; the distant light becomes a
train; clacking windows aglow, old faces
young faces male faces female faces
clickclack, gone; he turns green back to red
and continues to search the track for
irregularities—

Poet: "Hence, wreathed derailment. Casey Jones's
laughing skull, the last puff of steam, the last
wheel spun, the last scream removed, coffee
taste like steel in the rescuer's mouth; the
silver night eye could not face it; throughout
the night it summoned many a black cloud to
erase it—

107

"Nightgirls in blackest leather. . . O loadsome stretches of future! Black polar cow at bay— Circle troops of Fate, earth-shaped Destiny, direct-death straight arrow, semi-circle crow, carrion-edged ring, spiral mortification, gas-rings glued on gas-rings trim and narrow gas-tube. . . Sedentary diadem— Inself-hydra, infant many mouthed, and only one teat; no wonder the spirit-beest defines its own—"

BODY FISHED FROM THE SEINE

He floats down the Seine
The last victim of the FLN
He's Arab, he's soft, he's green
"He's a long time in the water been"
They're dragging him up now
Rope around his waist against the prow
Like a wet sponge he bounces and squirts
Somehow you feel though dead it hurts

I turned to Allen & Peter—what amazed them
Was not so much the sad victim
But how a big glass-top tourist boat
Stopped and had the tourists take note
They fresh from Eiffel and Notre-Dame
—A break of camera calm

A FRENCH BOY'S SUNDAY

Clean are our Sunday clothes,
we must take care not to dirty them!
Today's church day a rainy day O what a bad day!
Angel, with your chomping on white apples,
your wings are dipping in the muddy rain
O don't shake them, don't splatter our clothes
else our mother pull our ears!

Oh the Paris pissoirs on a cold rainy Sunday!
How lonely and damp and hard,
no love in the pissoirs!
And the grey pigeons all wet and hunched,
steamy iron and street-stone oppression,
careless ledges and pediments under which birds soak,
and splash their milky dung on the churchyard green,
the soggy dungy nobody-gives-a-goddam green!

Look at those old ones whispering hates
between their prayers and medicines;
that's what it's like every Sunday,
no love! no hope! then awful back-to-school Monday!
What is there to pray about outside, for all their tears,
          the poor pissoirs
must contend with our wines, Pschitt, and fears.

I DREAM IN THE DAYTIME

I dream in daytime
    much too somber
  to greet the angels
        at my velvet-shredded door

They enter salt
  they pour my milk
    they sprinkle white flies on the floor

I cringe my sink
  I gloom my stove

They leave me pink
    I dip my glove

GOD IS A MASTURBATOR

Folks, sex has never been
more than a blend
of bodies doing for one
another
that which pleases
them and evolution
to do
either in desire
or in desperation
or in necessity
It serves no purpose
other than love
and life's purpose
Sexualists
are a product of sex
We are made by sex
Sex made the Salvation Army
We are sex
There is nothing dark
about this magic
And those pangs of lust
which make you sick
Those unthinkable dreams
which fill you with doubt
—as long as wild joys emit
from an enthusiastic spirit
eat the dust! *shout!*
Thank God one's thoughts
excite as much as flesh
Thank God there's a place
in all this he and she
and he and he
and she and she
for a me and me—

ODE TO OLD ENGLAND & ITS LANGUAGE

To express what's seen, what's heard, imagined,
      dreamed,
to hear, to read, to write, to speak—curse, console,
      weep, laugh, O hybrid responsible irresponsible
champion of idea, lie, truth, platitudes, battered jargon,
      giant & dwarf altongue—
Paragnosis, splacturion, Spirit of the Barns, E A G L M D S,
    O silver alphabet in joy full return
to every tribe fresh and raw, clothed in animal,
      scamping swamps and forests, bear-baiting,
      firth-skimping, death-brothering,
to Gaels hording across the August bar;
    the Damnonian dusky promontory haycocking,
      setting hammer,
breast-rattling sun-shrieked beakers & horners, Cantii,
    massed visage, Wotin, hark! The England stretches
    away.

Bygone service, settlement mighty and sure,
    Trinobantes herald toward Essex, Middlesex,
      directionward;
      Iceni to Norfolk, Suffolk;
Cassii to Herts, Bucks, Bedford, onward; Coritani beaconed;
    Brigantes angled, and lo, the Belgae
      set their tents for settlement's end—
The memories of all the years of that beginning,
      the hunting, the hawking,
      weaponed men and free-necked men;
   ,thed in red and blue, bandaged crossways from
    ıkle to knee,
    the horned hat, the fierce braids and whiskers,
      fur smell, rawflesh shields;
chiefs dreaming heaven a vast hunt and feast,
      fearing hell an endless 4th season;
    and ladies in tight bodices fasten their mantles
      with wrought butterflies.

Tew, Freya, Saeter, the coming of Eostre;
the Mawy Clod's wolf-head ransom lain in the barrows,
    cromlechs;
            the Witena-gemot gathered in tribune,
                dole of free grain;
            theowes from frocland and bocland; than and
                ceorl;
Cyning and Etheling; sing, old vate, sing,
            wheat, barley, oat, rye, breathe the pastoral
                advance,
                all blast brown red yellow orange,
            sheep, cattle, swine, hardy tiller, earthbearer,
        soilwomber, kings & knights whistle across your fields;
lulled by firelight in your wicker domicile
            dreamed you chainless gold on the wrists of men?
                Good old Albion,
                    crib of liberty.

        Stonemeet oaken Druids teaching and judging,
their rite-drenched fingers directed toward the sun, moon,
    fire, water;
        splendors of wrong medicine, the laughing snake,
human spirits in the mice-clouds which veil the owl's brain;
dominion dance of brown-thoughts, skull-drink to compass
    the eye;
            Uraeus, Uraeus, loom from the East, rise, climb, bend,
                manifest each human sacrifice; summon a new
                magic,
a noumenal rune; drop harmless toothwort on the salver—
            And sat Caesar, as all waiting Decembers know,
                with burning head before the banks of Stour;
Cassivelaunus gathering clan after clan, all enjoinment,
                Briton entire;
yet destiny holds more than the ephemeral alliance of
    seasons and men;
        the brave tears of so early a nation fell,
        and falling stained all weathers hencefrom Verulam
—the sue for peace a vulnerable Argos never knew.

114

There be boars yet to spike; all's not grunting,
              wailing, woe;
look to Horsa at Aylesford, Danes belching mead in the yews;
        no echo of Ostorius facing Caradoc at Caer Caradoc,
but laughing Boadicea over osseous heaps of Rome;
              the palsied make path for William—
        Londinum rings; fall the Cheviots, the sacred oaks;
benevolent Agricola complete, all-eyed navigator,
                  'tis an isle, Albion's an isle;
                  hold it well,
fort the Firths of Forth and Clyde; wall Solway to the Tyne;
        friars outflock Mons Graupias;
                  bury Galgacus deep;
Carausius *Comes littoris Saxonica;* fall the Orkneys;
                  down Rome, down.

        Hail Britannia Prima, Britannia Secunda, Flavia,
        Maxima Caesariensis, Valentia, Vespasiana;
                  England full-named!
Eboracum to York, Camalodunum to Colchester, Thermae
        to Bath,
Isca Colonia to Caerleon, Rhutuple to Richborough—
        And the Venerable Bede bent in labor in God's
                  scriptorium,
              ignoring the abbot and his visitor in resplendent
              surcoat,
to record a Caedmonian hymn, England's first poem—
        And King Alfred the Encourager building abbeys and
              schools;
                  old Albion closes;
England opens, "Lo! we have listened to many a lay
              Of the Spear-Danes' fame, their splendors
              of old,
              Their mighty princes and martial deeds—"

IMMUTABLE MOODS

The rain
How it rings
    the chopped streets
    the umbrellad bicycles
    the tires of cars
And the trees
How they terrace it
and the roofs
How they avalanche it
  So dark and sog!
yet how lovely
      the feel of it
    and the sound!: Peet
  please pit peet please pit

        •

On darkest night
  a cloaked man reeling
  a woman putting coins
    in a cigarette machine—
What is it on darkest dark
  with bells and
      the trains of a slow night
a cloaked man lying still,
a woman smoking—

        •

What make of day!
Quickly into tunnels I run
  Huddling there
  a-tremble
    eyes darting how and where—
I called on old dead gods
  Bade them black out
    blot out complete
—O white!

·

Days and days of snow
Starched air, nurses, children,
        navies;
    I would communion go-O!
Come nights of fire!
    I can't face the stiff blanche day
ah dark bad fire
    ah still the day
Blacken useless destruction
    all remains
    I shan't go out
    Sit in my room in my gloom
        and laugh out my night
—Dawn
        I strangled the cock
        and walked into day
            Sun! Sun! Sun!

·

Knelt and heavened a child again
    Praying to an ignored flower
        Sun and green
            cows and brook
    O why do I cringe for night
        fanged wolves and gloopy
                        castles—

·

And I raised my hand
        that all stop
    and all stopped
        falling back
I lowered it not
    held it till all read thereon
        the folly of my duty
My fingers peeled like bananas
    and my palm burst like the sun

117

And yet I held
        bone knuckles full
and all all fell to their knees
    crying "It sees! It sees!"

.

Time geometrics sneaking in and out
        bona fide dimensions
Enunciating and commencing
        space expansions
—In extremis, cold April, Fichte,
Schelling, the relay is cumbrous and obscure
—unconverging infinite, inductile
        stretch, leagues—
    sublimity of distance and proximity
—Transmutations manifesting
    a metallic apotheosis
measureless, bountiful,
    and with no volitancy
—In extremis, Fichte, Hegel,
    Cold April

.

"Yet with you, A—you who so well
    know my toils— I rejoice
    as though the world were
    extorting heaven— glory, glory,
    in the lowest, the lips of angels,
    the curative properties of saints,
    with you, A, yet with you,
    O energy of existence, incarnate,
    dissolving, the contact crystallized,
    the axis negate,
    momentous conveyance abeyant,
        exact state, glory, glory,
        as well in the highest,
            the kiss of angels,
            the humanity of saints—"

118

·

Does it go to say Purgatory
    is with calendar and clock?
With doubt I am
        what times its measure
The doctrine of metempsychosis
The bleak illustration which dreams
        contribute to that tenet
What judge impose the credulity of it?
O doubtful sentence
O doubtful token of irresistibilities
    Penanced to the devil-choir
        mutable and transferable
    Whenever the half-doomed voice
            breaks
                into the angel-choir

·

    To ride a subway through
            a depth of purple glass
    To see intoxicly through
        a decanter of red wine
    To absorb the form of color
        in an infant's face
    To revolt against enamels
    To sustain only the purest color
        and maintain the sustenance. . .
Black may be the treasure of Nothingness
    O bleak molten creak
        what might have been
        what might have been seen!
    Red forks   yellow towers   pink Woten
            a train thru a decanter of red wine

·

Scampering shadows
a grunting Christ pointing toward an inhuman heaven
          Behold I too am a tree not for its leaves
Lumbered and carpentered a dilapidated shack
  in which I rock in a rocking chair
          like a man rocking in a rocking chair
       Swallowing this nothingness deviled me
Screaming a vast shipwreck
     strawdrawing a sea into a valley
and neither gifted with fear
nor exercised to save
     this madness dear
Behold behold I too

New Directions Paperbooks—A Partial Listing

For complete listing request free catalog from
New Directions, 80 Eighth Avenue, New York 10011

†Bilingual

Y. Mishima, *Confessions of a Mask.* NDP253.
  Death in Midsummer. NDP215.
Frédéric Mistral, *The Memoirs.* NDP632.
Eugenio Montale, *It Depends.*† NDP507.
  Selected Poems.† NDP193.
Paul Morand, *Fancy Goods / Open All Night.*
  NDP567.
Vladimir Nabokov, *Nikolai Gogol.* NDP78.
  Laughter in the Dark. NDP729.
  The Real Life of Sebastian Knight. NDP432.
P. Neruda, *The Captain's Verses.*† NDP345.
  Residence on Earth.† NDP340.
New Directions in Prose & Poetry (Anthology).
  Available from #17 forward to #55.
Robert Nichols, *Arrival.* NDP437.
  Exile. NDP485.
J. F. Nims, *The Six-Cornered Snowflake.* NDP700.
Charles Olson, *Selected Writings.* NDP231.
Toby Olson, *The Life of Jesus.* NDP417.
  Seaview. NDP532.
George Oppen, *Collected Poems.* NDP418.
István Örkeny, *The Flower Show /*
  The Toth Family. NDP536.
Wilfred Owen, *Collected Poems.* NDP210.
José Emilio Pacheco, *Battles in the Desert.* NDP637.
  Selected Poems.† NDP638.
Nicanor Parra, *Antipoems: New & Selected.* NDP603.
Boris Pasternak, *Safe Conduct.* NDP77.
Kenneth Patchen, *Because It Is.* NDP83.
  Collected Poems. NDP284.
  Selected Poems. NDP160.
  Wonderings. NDP320.
Ota Pavel, *How I Came to Know Fish.* NDP713.
Octavio Paz, *Collected Poems.* NDP719.
  Configurations.† NDP303.
  A Draft of Shadows.† NDP489.
  Selected Poems. NDP574.
  Sunstone.† NDP735.
  A Tree Within.† NDP661.
St. John Perse, *Selected Poems.*† NDP545.
J. A. Porter, *Eelgrass.* NDP438.
Ezra Pound, *ABC of Reading.* NDP89.
  Confucius. NDP285.
  Confucius to Cummings. (Anth.) NDP126.
  A Draft of XXX Cantos. NDP690.
  Elektra. NDP683.
  Guide to Kulchur. NDP257.
  Literary Essays. NDP250.
  Personae. NDP697.
  Selected Cantos. NDP304.
  Selected Poems. NDP66.
  The Spirit of Romance. NDP266.
Raymond Queneau, *The Blue Flowers.* NDP595.
  Exercises in Style. NDP513.
Mary de Rachewiltz, *Ezra Pound.* NDP405.
Raja Rao, *Kanthapura.* NDP224.
Herbert Read, *The Green Child.* NDP208.
P. Reverdy, *Selected Poems.*† NDP346.
Kenneth Rexroth, *An Autobiographical Novel.* NDP725.
  Classics Revisited. NDP621.
  More Classics Revisited. NDP668.
  Flower Wreath Hill. NDP724.
  100 Poems from the Chinese. NDP192.
  100 Poems from the Japanese.† NDP147.
  Selected Poems. NDP581.
  Women Poets of China. NDP528.
  Women Poets of Japan. NDP527.
Rainer Maria Rilke, *Poems from*
  The Book of Hours. NDP408.
  Possibility of Being. (Poems). NDP436.
  Where Silence Reigns. (Prose). NDP464.
Arthur Rimbaud, *Illuminations.*† NDP56.
  Season in Hell & Drunken Boat.† NDP97.
Edouard Roditi, *Delights of Turkey.* NDP445.
Jerome Rothenberg, *Khurbn.* NDP679.
  New Selected Poems. NDP625.
Nayantara Sahgal, *Rich Like Us.* NDP665.

Ihara Saikaku, *The Life of an Amorous*
  Woman. NDP270.
St. John of the Cross, *Poems.*† NDP341.
W. Saroyan, *Man With the Heart in the Highlands.*
  NDP740.
Jean-Paul Sartre, *Nausea.* NDP82.
  The Wall (Intimacy). NDP272.
P. D. Scott, *Coming to Jakarta.* NDP672.
  Listening to the Candle. NDP747.
Delmore Schwartz, *Selected Poems.* NDP241.
  In Dreams Begin Responsibilities. NDP454.
Shattan, *Manimekhalaï.* NDP674.
K. Shiraishi. *Seasons of Sacred Lust.* NDP453.
Stevie Smith, *Collected Poems.* NDP562.
  New Selected Poems. NDP659.
Gary Snyder, *The Back Country.* NDP249.
  The Real Work. NDP499.
  Regarding Wave. NDP306.
  Turtle Island. NDP381.
Muriel Spark, *The Public Image.* NDP767.
Enid Starkie, *Rimbaud.* NDP254.
Stendhal. *Three Italian Chronicles.* NDP704.
Antonio Tabucchi, *Indian Nocturne.* NDP666.
Nathaniel Tarn, *Lyrics . . . Bride of God.* NDP391.
Dylan Thomas, *Adventures in the Skin Trade.*
  NDP183.
  A Child's Christmas in Wales. NDP181.
  Collected Poems 1934-1952. NDP316.
  Collected Stories. NDP626.
  Portrait of the Artist as a Young Dog. NDP51.
  Quite Early One Morning. NDP90.
  Under Milk Wood. NDP73.
Tian Wen: A Chinese Book of Origins. NDP624.
Uwe Timm, *The Snake Tree.* NDP686.
Lionel Trilling, *E. M. Forster.* NDP189.
Tu Fu, *Selected Poems.* NDP675.
N. Tucci, *The Rain Came Last.* NDP688.
Paul Valéry, *Selected Writings.*† NDP184.
Elio Vittorini, *A Vittorini Omnibus.* NDP366.
Rosmarie Waldrop, *The Reproduction of Profiles.*
  NDP649.
Robert Penn Warren, *At Heaven's Gate.* NDP588.
Vernon Watkins, *Selected Poems.* NDP221.
Eliot Weinberger, *Outside Stories.* NDP751.
Nathanael West, *Miss Lonelyhearts &*
  Day of the Locust. NDP125.
J. Wheelwright, *Collected Poems.* NDP544.
Tennessee Williams, *Baby Doll.* NDP714.
  Camino Real. NDP301.
  Cat on a Hot Tin Roof. NDP398.
  Clothes for a Summer Hotel. NDP556.
  The Glass Menagerie. NDP218.
  Hard Candy. NDP225.
  A Lovely Sunday for Creve Coeur. NDP497.
  One Arm & Other Stories. NDP237.
  Red Devil Battery Sign. NDP650.
  A Streetcar Named Desire. NDP501.
  Sweet Bird of Youth. NDP409.
  Twenty-Seven Wagons Full of Cotton. NDP217.
  Vieux Carre. NDP482.
William Carlos Williams,
  The Autobiography. NDP223.
  The Buildup. NDP259.
  Collected Poems: Vol. I. NDP730
  Collected Poems: Vol. II. NDP731
  The Doctor Stories. NDP585.
  Imaginations. NDP329.
  In the American Grain. NDP53.
  In the Money. NDP240.
  Paterson. Complete. NDP152.
  Pictures from Brueghel. NDP118.
  Selected Poems (new ed.). NDP602.
  White Mule. NDP226.
Wisdom Books: *Spanish Mystics.* NDP442;
  St. Francis. NDP477; *Taoists.* NDP509;
  Wisdom of the Desert. NDP295;
  Zen Masters. NDP415.

For complete listing request free catalog from
New Directions, 80 Eighth Avenue, New York 10011   †Bilingual